HICKORYDICKORY

Marisa Wegrzyn

I0139605

BROADWAY PLAY PUBLISHING INC
New York
www.broadwayplaypublishing.com
info@broadwayplaypublishing.com

First edition: May 2018
I S B N: 978-0-88145-773-5

Book design: Marie Donovan
Page make-up: Adobe InDesign
Typeface: Palatino

HICKORYDICKORY was the winner of the 2009 Wendy Wasserstein Playwriting Prize.

HICKORYDICKORY premiered at Chicago Dramatists (Russ Tutterow, Artistic Director) in Chicago, running from 5 May–11 June 2011. The cast and creative contributors were as follows:

JIMMY/RICHARD.. Thomas Gebbia
KATE/HELEN .... Gail Rastorfer
DALE/YOUNG KATE.................................. Cathlyn Melvin
ROWAN/YOUNG JIMMY .... Tyler Ross
CARI LEE.. Joanne Dubach

Director ....Russ Tutterow
Scenic design... Simon Lashford
Lighting design ....Jeff Pines
Sound design.. Barry Bennett
Costume design ....Samantha Jones
Blood effects.. Ryan Oliver
Stage manager...Jennifer J Thusing

CHARACTERS

Each character pairing is played by a single actor. 5 actors total.

JIMMY, *ACT ONE and ACT THREE, male, 35.*
RICHARD, *ACT TWO, male, 40s.* JIMMY's *father.*

KATE, *ACT ONE and ACT THREE, female, 35.*
HELEN, *ACT TWO, female, 40s.* JIMMY's *mother.*

DALE, *ACT ONE and ACT THREE, female, 17.* CARI LEE *and* JIMMY's *daughter.*
KATE, *ACT TWO, female, 17.*

ROWAN, *ACT ONE and ACT THREE, male, early 20s. Irish, with an accent.*
JIMMY, *ACT TWO, male, 17.*

CARI LEE, *female, 17.*

SETTING

Wicker's Watch & Clock Repair shop in a northern suburb of Chicago. The shop is filled with clocks and display cases of watches. There's a workbench cluttered with tools, parts. Drawers in the wall. There's an easy chair perfect for napping, and a coat-rack by the door. The shop has an old lived-in feel about it, a place with lots of nooks and crannies. There is access to the Wicker's upstairs apartment from a staircase or an inside exit in the shop. Exiting the shop to the outdoors is a portion of the sidewalk with a bench. A large shop window looks out onto this bench and sidewalk. A sign in the window of the shop glows: WATCH & CLOCK REPAIR.

Time:

ACT ONE—Spring, the present

ACT TWO—Spring, 18 years earlier

ACT THREE—The present and past

ACT ONE

Scene 1
A Girl & Her Favorite Sheep

(Morning in the Watch & Clock Repair shop. JIMMY works on a clock. The phone rings.)

JIMMY: *(On phone:)* Wicker's Watch and Clock repair, this is Jimmy.
*

Good morning, Mrs Herman.
*

No, no, I'm not Richard—I'm Jimmy. His son. That's okay.
*

I'm still waiting on the parts, takes a long time, I'll call you as soon as—
*

Germany.
*

Germany, it's a German watch.
*

I can pester them to hurry up but then they yell at me. In German. It's scary.
*

I like all kinds of strudel!

(KATE and DALE enter, mid-conversation, from upstairs. DALE has her backpack. JIMMY will occasionally qualify

his end of the phone conversation with an "mm hmm" but mostly covers the mouthpiece with his hand)

KATE: But you keep putting me in this awkward situation when you don't do the assignments like everybody else. It's an AP class, Dale.

DALE: Sorry, sorry, okay, what do you want me to do?

KATE: Do the reading, that's a start.

JIMMY: *(Covers the phone)* What's going on?

DALE: I'm supposed to lead discussion today.

KATE: She didn't finish the reading.

JIMMY: Why didn't you finish the reading?

DALE: I forgot.

JIMMY: Just because Kate's your teacher doesn't mean you can forget when you don't feel like doing your homework.

KATE: Did you look at the dishwasher like you said you would?

JIMMY: I forgot. But that's not because I didn't feel like it, it's because I forgot.

DALE: You know I don't like talking in class.

(KATE fusses with DALE's hair.)

KATE: You don't have to talk much. Ask some good questions and the windbags will commandeer the discussion but don't tell Jeff and Trina I called them windbags.

(DALE smiles.)

KATE: You have a pretty face and a nice smile. *When* you smile. I saw this really cute shirt at The Gap last week that would look great on you, seriously. And it wasn't—what did you call that one shirt?

DALE: Boob-a-licious.

KATE: No, the other one.

DALE: Skank-tastic.

KATE: It wasn't skank-tastic, it was very *you*. We should go shopping. We'll buy Frappuccinos. It'll be fun. *(She gets a lipstick out of her bag.)* Go like this:

(KATE makes a lipstick-receiving face. She'll put some lipstick on DALE.)

DALE: Dad, Kate is trying to tart me up again. Make her stop.

JIMMY: Oh, Kiddo, I'd like to help, but this is a very important phone call. *(Phone:)* My head says chocolate strudel, but my stomach says apple. How about you surprise me when I swing by to pick it up. Bye now. *(Hangs up)* All right. No more stalling. What do you want for your birthday?

DALE: Stop asking me that.

JIMMY: What do you want for your birthday?

KATE: You can have anything you want.

JIMMY: Within reason.

KATE: Do you want a car?

JIMMY: *(To KATE)* Maybe we should define the term "within reason".

KATE: You're turning eighteen. Kind of a big deal.

DALE: It's not a big deal.

JIMMY: It's okay to want something.

DALE: I don't want anything.

(ROWAN enters the shop with coffee cups for JIMMY and KATE.)

ROWAN: Morning all.

JIMMY: Morning, Rowan.

ROWAN: Mrs Wicker, Dale.

KATE: Oh, please—

ROWAN: Call you Kate. Right. Kate. I think I got it right, like you told me yesterday. Your man at the shop knew your drinks, so I didn't even have to remember. But I did remember if he hadn't known, or, like, if he's not there tomorrow.

KATE: Thanks, Rowan.

ROWAN: Anything new today?

JIMMY: The Breitling for Mr Montour, and my buddy Greg's bringing in a Viennese 3 Weight.

KATE: Please don't bring Greg upstairs.

JIMMY: My friends are allowed in our home.

DALE: Dad, he smells like cheese.

KATE: *(To* DALE*)* You ready? Oh—the acceptance letter to mail.

DALE: Nah.

KATE: Wh— "nah"? What does that mean, "nah"?

DALE: I'm not going to college.

JIMMY: Umm, no, that's incorrect.

DALE: You didn't go to college.

JIMMY: Because I was busy changing your diapers.

DALE: I'm not ready to go.

KATE: You're more than ready. You're the best writer in the class. Math Department Steve says you're acing A P Calc like it's no big deal. You'll love Northwestern. Dale, you can't keep acting like life doesn't continue beyond high school.

(Pause)

DALE: I don't need a ride. I'm gonna read a few more pages before I go. I'll try to be ready for discussion today.

JIMMY: Don't be late for school. It's embarrassing, you live above a clock shop and you're always late.

DALE: Right, Dad.

(DALE *gives* JIMMY *a kiss on the cheek leaving a lipstick smooch mark*)

JIMMY: *(Kinda touched)* What was that for?

DALE: Just trying to get this lipstick off.

JIMMY: Glad I could be of service.

(JIMMY *and* KATE *exit the shop and stand outside.* KATE *gets some Kleenex to wipe her nose—checking on the final stages of an earlier nose bleed)*

JIMMY: What's this "I'm not going to college" business? Where'd that come from?

KATE: She's nervous about change.

JIMMY: It's not that big a change. Northwestern's five minutes away, she can live at home if she wants. And I don't understand how she could not want anything for her birthday. When I was her age, I *wanted*. I wanted *stuff*. I wanted everything. She's too young to hate birthdays.

KATE: I hate birthdays.

JIMMY: You love birthdays.

KATE: I love *birthday cake*. The getting older thing is attached to the excitement of the cake thing. Collateral excitement.

JIMMY: You need more Kleenex?

KATE: I'm good. *(She wipes the lipstick smooch mark off* JIMMY's *face.)* Lovely color on you. Lipstick.

JIMMY: I'm more a Viva Glam Red kinda guy.

KATE: Why is that something you know?

JIMMY: I have many secrets.

KATE: Are you ever going to let me in on your secrets?

JIMMY: Mmmmyes. I'm in love with a dwarf.

KATE: Oh stop it.

JIMMY: Her charisma, her dexterity, her dice have cast a spell on me. Her name is Rosalind, the sweetest dwarf in all the land. She's stolen my heart and now I want her to have my Halfling wizard babies.

KATE: We're too old for Dungeons & Dragons foreplay.

JIMMY: Not if it still makes you tingle. Come on. … What?

KATE: The baby thing.

JIMMY: I thought we could talk about it again.

KATE: Last night you made it sound like it was our sole responsibility to repopulate a dying planet, like, RIGHT NOW.

JIMMY: You're making me feel like an insensitive jerk if that's really what it sounded like.

KATE: You're not a jerk.

JIMMY: But I'm insensitive.

KATE: Jimmy, in certain matters, you can be…

JIMMY: Insensitive.

KATE: No.

JIMMY: Pushy.

KATE: (Thinking) Mmm.

JIMMY: What?

KATE: Aggressively optimistic.

JIMMY: That's not a bad thing.

KATE: It's a *thing*.

JIMMY: It's not a thing that's a bad thing.

KATE: It's a thing that plucked a nerve. And I didn't mean to *go off* at you, if that's what it sounded like. We're both striking out with the hyperbole.

JIMMY: Remind me again?

KATE: Exaggeration.

JIMMY: Right.

KATE: I'm going to make an appointment with Dr Olmhurst. See if she can squeeze me in this week. Do you want to come?

JIMMY: Of course, yes, if you want me to.

(KATE readies her car keys. KATE exits first, and JIMMY lingers a moment looking in the shop. DALE looks up at JIMMY. He gestures to the watch on his wrist. DALE begins packing up her things for school. JIMMY exits.)

ROWAN: Watch this. *(He tries to toss his hat onto the coat rack from where he's sitting.)* I do like a good standing coat rack. I don't know why. Pegs on the wall do save room if you're worried about clutter, but there's something about getting home dropping your hat and hanging your coat on one. Or seeing it out of the corner of your eye as a dressed up person. Not a talker, but always there for a bit of company. Anyway. *(He returns to his work.)*

DALE: Rowan? Has my dad taught you about pocket watches, fixing pocket watches?

ROWAN: I've worked on a few.

DALE: Do you think you could fix this?

(DALE gets a pocket watch from her backpack and hands it to ROWAN)

ROWAN: Engraved, very nice. *Cari Lee?*

DALE: Cari Lee. My mom. My real mom.

ROWAN: Is Cari Lee, em... gone?

DALE: She's gone but not, like, dead-gone. She was
seventeen when she had me and then she just left.
...I don't even have, like, a photo of her. Kate had
this one picture someone took of her and some of
her cheerleading friends in high school. Kate in a
cheerleading uniform with all the other cheerleaders
with big horse teeth. Cari Lee was the one in the
background, out of focus. Slouching against the
lockers, giving the cheerleaders the finger. *(She
demonstrates* CARI LEE's *pose)*

ROWAN: I knew a girl like that my year of school in
Dublin. She'd have none of me though. Thought I was
a dull bog-trotter when I wasn't that far out of Dublin
meself, but. She in her leather and the boots and mud
spattered legs, Ah, well. The way it is sometimes.
There's well worse things than being thought dull.

DALE: I don't think you're dull.

ROWAN: No? Are you sure, now?

DALE: I'm a connoisseur of dull. You're not dull.

ROWAN: Ahh, go on out of that now. Ya haven't gotten
to know me. I'll be putting you into a coma before the
day is up, you'll be all: *(Makes a drooling limp lipped
zombie face)*

*(*DALE *smiles, laughs.)*

ROWAN: You didn't know your mother, but I'd say
she was a beautiful girl if she looked anything like her
daughter.

DALE: *(Blushes)* Sure. Right.

*(*ROWAN *takes a photograph from his wallet, shows* DALE*)*

ROWAN: Me own mother when she was a little girl. Her and her favorite sheep.

DALE: I wish I was from a place where I could have a favorite sheep.

ROWAN: Right, I don't see too many sheep wandering down the road here. I didn't know her, either. She's gone now. Dead. Me mother I mean, not the sheep. Or the sheep's gone as well, I'm sure, as sheep tend to go.

DALE: How did your mother die?

ROWAN: It's a bit maudlin. I don't mind telling if you do want to know, like. When I was a little boy, me mother was very unhappy and she killed herself. Put a gun to her own chest. This is how I like to remember her *(Photo)*. In a way I would never've known her. As a happy girl with a favorite sheep. *(He looks at* CARI LEE's *pocket watch.)* Funny for a lady to have a pocket watch. It's beautiful. Has a weight about it, but it's not heavy, you know? It's unusual.

DALE: Do you think you can fix it?

ROWAN: I can open it, sure. But I'm still learning. Your father would know better than I. You should have him do it for you.

DALE: No. He doesn't know I found it.

ROWAN: Ohh. I wouldn't feel right working on this without his permission.

DALE: It's just been sitting in a box inside a shoebox behind some stuff in his closet. It's the only thing he's kept of her. It would mean a lot for this thing of my mom's to not be broken, you know? I want somebody to fix it.

(ROWAN prepares to open the watch.)

ROWAN: Do you drink coffee, Dale? If your father sends me out for coffee and if you want something I'd like to know what to get for you.

DALE: You don't have to do that.

ROWAN: Oh. But I'd like to. Or. Would ever you'd like to go to The Bean Counter sometime?

DALE: Um. What, like a date?

ROWAN: It wouldn't have to be today. At any sort of convenience.

DALE: I don't really...date.

ROWAN: We wouldn't have to call it that. We could call it a...coat rack. The two of us will go on a coat rack.

DALE: I don't go on coat racks.

ROWAN: I do enjoy your company. That's all. Thought I'd ask if you had an evening free, say, this Friday evening and it wouldn't have to be late, like. If you'd be wanting a bite to eat, we could do that, or not. It's all right if you don't want to. Thought I'd ask.

DALE: It's not that I don't want to. I shouldn't get too close to people. It'll just make everything really difficult.

ROWAN: I don't understand.

DALE: If I tell you, you'll think I'm, like, totally nuts. You'll think I'm crazy-nuts. Like, straight-jacket loony.

ROWAN: I won't think that.

DALE: Do you promise you won't tell anybody?

ROWAN: If it's that important to you, I promise.

(Pause)

DALE: I know when I'm going to die.

ROWAN: You know when you're going to die? ...How
would you be knowing a thing like that? ...Why do
you say that, Dale?

DALE: Nevermind.

ROWAN: Dale.

DALE: I can't be late for school. I can't be late. *(She is
almost out the door, stops:)* Friday. Okay. Okay. Yes. I'll
go on a coat rack with you on Friday. That would be...
really nice.

*(DALE exits. ROWAN looks at CARI LEE's pocket watch and
sits down at the workbench with it. ROWAN opens up CARI
LEE's pocket watch and sticks a tool in it. Blood spurts and
drips from the watch)*

ROWAN: Jaysus!

Scene 2
Internal Defects & Dangling Chains

*(A few days later. DALE is alone in the shop doing
homework. Outside the shop, CARI LEE enters. She's
seventeen years old; exciting, vulgar, flamboyant, etc. She
enters the shop.)*

CARI LEE: Hi.

DALE: Hi. We're closed.

CARI LEE: Is Jimmy here?

DALE: He's at an appointment.

*(CARI LEE looks at the coat rack, laughs, picks it up and
moves it)*

DALE: Uhh. Can I help you?

CARI LEE: I dunno *caaaaan* you?

DALE: Like I said, we're closed.

CARI LEE: Then what are you doing here?

DALE: I'm just doing homework.

(CARI LEE looks at DALE up and down, fascinated)

DALE: What?

CARI LEE: Calculus, huh? That stuff is hard, man. You think that stuff's hard? That stuff's hard. I was never smart enough to get it. I was in Math Fundamentals. But we all called it Math Fun-For-Mentals. You wanna see the one thing I learned in that class? *(She grabs DALE's calculator.)* 55378008. And then you turn it upside down. *(Shows the calculator to DALE)*

DALE: Boobless.

CARI LEE: Boobless! You get good grades?

DALE: Yeah.

CARI LEE: Awesome. Awesome. Yeah, 'cause like, don't go through this world being stupid. Be as smart as you can or one day you may wind up looking for your flip-flops in the dumpster behind the Dairy Queen wondering what the hell you did last night. *(She puts down the calculator.)* Maybe you can help me.

DALE: Mmm probably not.

CARI LEE: I'm looking for a watch.

DALE: We have many.

CARI LEE: I'm looking for a very very special watch. A pocket watch.

DALE: Did you bring it in to get it repaired?

CARI LEE: Has my name engraved on it.

DALE: What's the name?

CARI LEE: Cari Lee.

(Pause)

DALE: Cari Lee?

(CARI LEE *beams.*)

DALE: No.

CARI LEE: Yes.

DALE: You're not. You can't be her.

CARI LEE: Why not?

DALE: You're too young to be her.

CARI LEE: So.

DALE: How old are you?

CARI LEE: I'm seventeen.

DALE: But—*I'm* seventeen

CARI LEE: Uh huh.

DALE: So my mom has to be 34 almost 35.

CARI LEE: What's your point?

DALE: My point is my mom had me when *she* was seventeen so you are not my mom.

CARI LEE: *(Darth Vader:) Dale. I am your mother.*

DALE: I want to see some I D. Some photo identification.

(CARI LEE *dumps her bag on the counter. Assorted junk. C D cases, make-up, a set of drumsticks, a bunch of lollypops.*)

CARI LEE: Man oh man I got a lotta crap in here—Oh. Here. Lookit. *(Shows* DALE *a Polaroid picture)* That's the day after you were born. Me and you and Jimmy and Mr and Mrs Wicker. I guess you never knew them.

DALE: No.

CARI LEE: Sucks what happened to them.

DALE: What happened to them?

CARI LEE: You don't know?

DALE: Well…I know they died. Is that what you mean?

(A pause. This is not something CARI LEE *wants to get in to.)*

CARI LEE: Yeah. Yeah. ...I like that picture. You can't keep it, though. It's the only one I got.

DALE: That's you and... that's my dad. He's so skinny!

CARI LEE: Oh no way, did Jimmy get fat?

DALE: He just doesn't look like this anymore.

CARI LEE: I don't gain weight. Not one ounce. I can eat anything. *(Gets a ribbon out of her bag)* I won the first place ribbon in a pie eating contest last summer. Beat all these fat dudes. It ruled.

DALE: How is this possible?

CARI LEE: Oh, it all just comes out the other end.

DALE: I don't understand what's going on.

CARI LEE: All's you need to understand is we're supposed to love each other! We're just supposed to know we love each other because you are my spawn. Do you do drugs?

DALE: No.

CARI LEE: Pot?

DALE: I said I don't do drugs.

CARI LEE: Pot's not a *drug* drug, it's recreation, like tennis. I used to do drugs but drugs are only fun until your dog eats your last bag of coke, and then you have to get a new dog. You got a boyfriend?

DALE: No.

CARI LEE: You got a girlfriend?

DALE: No.

CARI LEE: Anybody you got a crush on? Is he or she cute? I missed everything about your life, just trying to play catch-up, Daleywaley.

DALE: Don't call me Daleywaley.

CARI LEE: Daleywaley babycakes.

(CARI LEE *tries giving* DALE *a hug.* DALE *evades.*)

DALE: What are you doing?

CARI LEE: I am giving you a hug.

DALE: Please don't. You smell like hippies.

CARI LEE: (*Smells herself*) It's not my natural scent, okay? I hitched a ride in this van with some friends of my band. I play drums. You play music?

DALE: No.

CARI LEE: My band is shellacked with the holy spirit of rock and roll. And Scooter is finally taking guitar lessons. Before he was always like, "Rock and roll can't be taught, it's in your *veins* and your *bones* and covers your soul in *gravy*" and then he picks up his guitar and proceeds to totally suck balls. It's like *unbelievable,* Scooter, I've heard farts more musical than that. (*She gets a C D from her stuff.*) The world premier demo of my band, Smack Dab & The Moist Toweletts:

(CARI LEE *puts her C D on the stereo. It's a lot of rock and roll noise and it sucks.*)

CARI LEE: Pretty good, huh? We rock!

(DALE *turns off the music.*)

CARI LEE: Can I ask you a serious question?

DALE: Okay.

CARI LEE: Is it totally weird to think you used to suck on my boobs?

DALE: I haven't really thought about it.

CARI LEE: Are you thinking about it now that I brought it up?

DALE: I'm trying not to.

CARI LEE: You sucked on my boobs and milk came out. I don't even *like* milk and it came *out of me*. For you! You should thank me.

DALE: But you didn't want me!

CARI LEE: Did Jimmy tell you that? Is that what he's been saying, that I didn't want you? Did he say that, 'cause it's not true.

(Outside the shop, KATE will enter and sit on the bench. She's squeezing her nose with a Kleenex, head back, tending another nose bleed.)

CARI LEE: *Oh my god.* No way. I totally know her! We were in the same homeroom. Nerdface, man, she was an uber-cheerleading-dork. And she'd get these crazy nose bleeds, man, like out of nowhere, just, gush. Is Jimmy still friends with her?

DALE: Kate's my step-mom.

CARI LEE: Kate's your—what? Whaaaaat? She and Jimmy, like… No way. For real?

DALE: Yeah.

CARI LEE: Do you like her?

DALE: I like her a lot.

CARI LEE: Did she read to you and take you to the zoo and stuff?

DALE: Yeah.

(Outside, JIMMY enters)

CARI LEE: Jimmy.

(JIMMY sits next to KATE. KATE removes the Kleenex. She wipes her nose with her fingers. JIMMY holds out a tissue.)

KATE: No, it's just crusty. *(Pause)* Dr Olmhurst is really great with breaking bad news, how bout that, huh? She should give lessons, teach a class.

JIMMY: It's not fair.

KATE: Well. It's not your fault. *(Pause)* This would be a good time for you to say it's not my fault either.

JIMMY: It's not your fault.

KATE: Wow, glad I yanked that gem of sincerity out of you.

JIMMY: It's not your fault. How else do you want me to say it?

KATE: I don't know.

JIMMY: Well I'm sorry, obviously I'm an idiot.

KATE: You're not an idiot.

JIMMY: Do you want to talk about maybe adopting?

KATE: Do you think I want to have that conversation now? Right now? Really?
Give me some time, okay, Jimmy? I just need some time.

CARI LEE: Do they have, like, other kids too?

DALE: They've been trying. I really want it to work out for them. I want... I want them to be happy when I'm gone.

(Pause)

CARI LEE: When are you gonna die? Soon? How soon? Years? Months? Days?

(CARI LEE tries approaching DALE out of some sort of maternal instinct. DALE backs away from her)

DALE: Don't touch me!

CARI LEE: You're not crazy, Dale. I know you probably thought you were alone in this. You're not crazy and you're not alone.

JIMMY: You want pizza for dinner?

KATE: Pizza and beer.

JIMMY: Six pack?

(Off KATE*'s look:)*

JIMMY: 12 pack.

*(*JIMMY *enters the shop. Looks at* CARI LEE. *Stunned)*

CARI LEE: Whatup bastard!

JIMMY: Oh my God.

*(*CARI LEE *jumps* JIMMY, *squeezes him, smears her face into his chest.)*

CARI LEE: Oh Jimmy! Jimmy Jimmy Jimmy. My little short stop Jimmybear. What *happened* to you? I know it's you but the feel of you and the *smell* of you is different …it's…Old Spice and coffee and lazy Sunday mornings reading the paper and taxes and the ozone smell of creaky knees, *ohhhh god, Jimmy.* You're old! And you haven't told Dale a damn thing! Not one damn thing about mortal clocks! She didn't know I was seventeen! That would've been a good thing to tell her, you think?! You dope! You crap head! You flop ass llama! So where is it, man? You got it, right? Where is it? Lemme see it, I know you were messing around with it.

JIMMY: Messing around with what?

CARI LEE: Dude: you opened my mortal clock.

JIMMY: But—I didn't.

CARI LEE: You didn't?

JIMMY: No.

CARI LEE: Somebody opened it! I felt it. I was banging on my drums in a garage when I felt that whoosh through my whole body and I thought it was you. C'mon, man, don't mess with me, I totally know you opened it!

JIMMY: I don't deal with mortal clocks! *(Beat)* Dale?

DALE: Yeah Dad?

JIMMY: Did you find a pocket watch? A pocket watch, with Cari Lee's name engraved on it?

DALE: Ummmmaybe.

JIMMY: What did you do with it?

DALE: I gave it to Rowan. To fix.

(JIMMY goes to the phone, dials.)

JIMMY: Why did you do that, Dale.

DALE: It was broken.

JIMMY: You shouldn't've gone through my things! *(On the phone:)* Rowan, hi. This is Jimmy Wicker. Dale said she gave you a pocket watch to work on.
*

Yes, it is an unusual watch—no, no I'm not angry with you. I'm not angry w—Rowan!—I'm not angry. I need you to bring that pocket watch back here as soon as you can.
*

What, what do you mean, what happened?
*

Okay, um, yes, do that, and um, *(Very quietly)* sponge up what you can. *(Hangs up)*

CARI LEE: Something wrong with my mortal clock?

(JIMMY looks a CARI LEE. Looks at KATE outside [who hasn't seen CARI LEE].)

JIMMY: Excuse me. *(He exits the shop and approaches KATE outside.)* It's been awhile since we've had a conversation about Cari Lee Bliley.

KATE: …? Okay?

JIMMY: I, uh. Found out where she is.

KATE: Really? Was I right? Waitressing at an Applebee's off the interstate?

JIMMY: No. Kate. Uh.

KATE: What's wrong?

JIMMY: Cari Lee was one of those people my parents helped.

(A pause—they never talk about this business)

KATE: You never told me that Cari Lee had her mortal clock removed.

JIMMY: I guess I forgot to tell you that.

KATE: "You forgot."

JIMMY: My parents removed her mortal clock from her head. And when we were seventeen years old, I broke her mortal clock. And she is still seventeen years old. And she is standing right behind us.

(KATE *turns to look inside the shop.* CARI LEE *is right behind them on the other side of the window. She smiles, waves, etc.* KATE *enters the shop followed by* JIMMY.*)*

CARI LEE: Tsup!

(Off KATE's *surprise:)*

CARI LEE: I know, right. I look great. It's cuz I moisturize. When's this Rowan guy getting here with my mortal clock?

KATE: You gave her mortal clock to *Rowan*?

JIMMY: Dale gave it to Rowan.

KATE: Why'd Dale have Cari Lee's mortal clock to give to *Rowan*?

CARI LEE: Why do you keep saying *Rowan* like that? Is he stupid? Does a stupid guy have my mortal clock?

JIMMY: He's an apprentice. He's learning.

KATE: You've had Cari Lee's mortal clock this whole time.

JIMMY: She left here without it, and I held on to it. I wasn't going to throw it away. And Rowan will be here soon with it.

DALE: Dad? Do I have a mortal clock?

(Pause)

JIMMY: Everybody has a mortal clock. Tucked behind the heart, hidden under the steady thump.

DALE: It knows when I'm going to die.

JIMMY: Yes. And it's for the best that people in this world don't know about their mortal clocks, okay?

DALE: It counts down the seconds to when I'm going to die.

KATE: Dale: you don't have to worry about it. Right, Jimmy? She doesn't have to worry. I don't worry about my mortal clock. You don't have to worry about yours.

JIMMY: You'll never hear it or see it and you'll never know what time it has.

CARI LEE: Welllllllllllllllll...some people know because they can hear their mortal clocks.

JIMMY: Yes, but we don't hear our mortal clocks because they're here. *(Taps chest)*

CARI LEE: Yes, but some people have them up here. *(Taps head)*

JIMMY: It's a rare condition.

CARI LEE: Dude, I'm just sayin it wouldn't be crazy if, say, Dale was born with her mortal clock in her head. Right?

JIMMY: And I'm sure Dale would have said something if she had heard something.

(They look to DALE. *She appears to have a headache—as if the sound in her head is amplified by knowing the truth)*

DALE: I'm sorry.

*(*KATE *goes to* DALE *to comfort her)*

KATE: Hey. Dale. Hey.

DALE: I'm so sorry I'm so so sorry I'm sorry I'm sorry.

KATE: Why are you sorry?

DALE: I know when I'm going to die.

(Pause)

KATE: How long have you known?

DALE: I can't remember not knowing. I'm sorry.

KATE: Don't be sorry. Dale? Don't be sorry. It'll be okay.

CARI LEE: Only way it'll be okay is if you get it out of her head.

JIMMY: No.

CARI LEE: Extraction.

JIMMY: Oh no.

CARI LEE: Oh yes! Extraction!

JIMMY: No.

CARI LEE: That's what happens now, yes! He can take it out of your head.

DALE: He can take it out?

JIMMY: Dale, taking it out doesn't stop it from ticking. You'll still die when it says you'll die. You'll still keep getting older.

DALE: Then how come Cari Lee's stopped? How come my mom is seventeen?

JIMMY: That was a different circumstance. Mortal clocks aren't supposed to stop.

CARI LEE: It's cruel to leave it in, man.

JIMMY: Extraction was my mom and dad's thing. I never did any of this on my own.

CARI LEE: Bet you saved their tools and potions and stuff. And your mom's book. Bet you couldn't throw that away.

DALE: I want it out of my head.
I want it out.
Dad, when you asked me what I wanted for my birthday? And I said I didn't want anything. And you said I could have anything. *Anything.* I want you to take this stupid clock out of my head. I don't want to hear when I'm going to die, please, please, please. Every second goes by and it's one more second til I die and it's all I hear. It's all I've ever heard. I'm dying every second.

JIMMY: No, you're living. This is living.

DALE: I wouldn't know. I've never heard it that way before.

JIMMY: I can't take it out.

DALE: GET IT OUT OF MY HEAD!!! I can't live like this anymore!

JIMMY: It's all right, sweetheart. It's going to be okay. You're going to be all right. All right? I know you're going to be all right.

KATE: Jimmy. How difficult is an extraction?

JIMMY: It can be difficult. It's been a long time since I helped my parents with one of these.

CARI LEE: He's a total pro.

(JIMMY *retrieves some long-stashed, hidden materials. A box with some tools and bottles and jars. And—a heavy book that lands with a thud on the work table*)

KATE: What's this?

JIMMY: My mom's book. Everything she knew about mortal clocks.

KATE: Can I read it? *(She reaches for it.)*

JIMMY: Don't! Please. *(Beat)* I thought this mortal clock business was over.

KATE: Is it ever really going to be over?

(JIMMY *opens the book. Allows* KATE *to look at it)*

DALE: Dad?

JIMMY: Yeah.

DALE: Is this gonna hurt?

CARI LEE: Oh my god yes!

JIMMY: Don't say that.

CARI LEE: Getting a mortal clock pulled outta your brain hurts like a mofo.

JIMMY: It's going to be a little uncomfortable.

CARI LEE: "A little uncomfortable" like a mofo but totally worth it. It'll be so quiet. You won't believe how quiet the world can be when you can't hear the seconds tick away.

(JIMMY *consults the text. He pours liquid from the bottles in the coffee mug. Tosses some powders in it. Stirs it)*

CARI LEE: Look at Harry Potter over there. Got an A in potions class.

JIMMY: Hold onto this, I'll explain when we get there—

(JIMMY *hands* KATE *a tangled-up leather strap.)*

JIMMY: Dale, you need to know that once I start the extraction, I can't stop. I can't do it halfway and stop. I need to know that this is absolutely what you want.

DALE: This is what I want.

JIMMY: Happy eighteenth birthday, kiddo. Cheers.

(JIMMY *hands* DALE *the mug.*)

DALE: What is this?

JIMMY: First it's going to make you feel really cold. Then you'll feel really really warm and your arms and legs and hands and feet will feel like jelly as it soaks into your brain. And the chain from your mortal clock drips down from your brain to a place I can reach— with this.

(JIMMY *shows* DALE *a big scary-looking hook.*)

DALE: You're going to stick that where?

JIMMY: It's just gonna go… *(Mimes the hook going into his throat)* …like that *(Twists the hook)* and then that. Do you still want to do this, Dale?

(DALE *drinks.*)

JIMMY: We just have to wait at little bit, let that soak in, and I have to uh, *(Flips through book),* study this out.

KATE: *(To* CARI LEE*)* Can we talk a minute?

CARI LEE: Okay.

KATE: Outside.

CARI LEE: Ohhhh *outside.* Hey Jimmy, me and Kate are gonna go outside and make out.

JIMMY: *(Got his attention)* Huh?

KATE: We'll be outside.

(KATE *and* CARI LEE *go outside the shop.*)

JIMMY: I'm going to remove your mortal clock. And I'm going to give it to you, put it in your own hands, it's *yours.* You need to put it in a very safe place. Make sure it stays safe and sound. Don't let anybody open it up and look at it.

DALE: Even you?

JIMMY: Even me.

(Outside the shop:)

CARI LEE: You get the surgery where they shave your eyeballs with lasers?

KATE: What?

CARI LEE: No more glasses.

KATE: Did Dale tell you how much time is left on her mortal clock?

CARI LEE: No.

KATE: Did you ask her?

CARI LEE: Yeah, she freaked.

KATE: So her time might be up soon?

CARI LEE: You really didn't know? I mean, it's hereditary. I'm not surprised that Dale didn't tell you she could hear it. When you know, you don't tell the people you love. It's the tick tick tick that gets you. There's more to each tick than just sound. It's like your skin gets heavier like wet clothes you can't take off. Your lungs fill and empty and you know exactly how many more times you'll get to sigh and laugh and cry. Nothing seems important because everything is important. You're lucky, Kate, you never had one in your head. Yours is safely, quietly, where it belongs *(Points to* KATE's *chest)* Thanks for being good to Dale.

KATE: You don't have to thank me for that.

CARI LEE: I didn't get Dale anything for her birthday coming up when she'll officially be, like, older than me. Like I haven't gotten her anything, ever. And now I feel this overwhelming urge to give, like this gassy urge to give and give. You know what Dale said she really wanted?

KATE: What?

CARI LEE: She wanted you and Jimmy to be happy.

KATE: She said that?

CARI LEE: Yeah, she did. And she's right. You and Jimmy should be happy.

KATE: That's really nice of you to say, Cari Lee.

CARI LEE: Yeah, I'm really nice, but like, I don't know how to give her what she wants, which is for you and Jimmy to be happy. Would a puppy make you happy? Let me thank you with puppies.

KATE: Do not thank me with puppies.

CARI LEE: You were there for my daughter, and I'm not leaving here until you are decently thanked so watch your back! I'm gonna drop an A-Bomb of Gratitude on your Los Alamos.

KATE: The only thing that will make me happy is for Dale to be okay.

(JIMMY *is gesturing for* CARI LEE *and* KATE *to come back in.*)

CARI LEE: Here we go. Ready?

(*And* CARI LEE *and* KATE *go in the shop.* DALE *is glassy-eyed, high.*)

DALE: I can feel my *feet* in my *shoes*. My feet are in my shoes. I have feet. Huhn.

CARI LEE: Jimmy: thank you for letting me be a part of my daughter's first high.

DALE: Cari *Leeeee.*

CARI LEE: You ready to have your world rocked, hot stuff?

DALE: My what forked?

JIMMY: *(To* KATE*)* Okay, you ready to help me with that? *(The leather strap)* I'm going to need you to hold her still. She's going to squirm.

CARI LEE: Squirm like a worm with a perm.

JIMMY: And this all may look unpleasant. But I need you to hold her tight, Kate. I need you to hold on to her for me. Don't let her go.

*(*CARI LEE *goes to the stereo. Looks through the stack of C Ds)*

CARI LEE: Any requests? Why does all this music totally blow. Manheim Steamroller? Are you kidding? *(Flings the C D, finds something else)* Here we go. Mix Master Cari Lee Bliley rolling out the rock in the little clock shop that don't stop.

*(*CARI LEE *picks a C D and puts it in the stereo. Maybe the operatic glam-rock of Queen's "Don't Stop Me Now" or the bubblegum rah-rah of The Beach Boys' "Be True To Your School" or Sweet's "Little Willy" or I don't know. Whatever it is, it's a little wacky and dissonant with* KATE *holding* DALE *down with a strap, and* JIMMY *sticking a hook down his daughter's throat. When* DALE *begins howling and squirming and kicking and twitching and fighting* KATE *holds tight,* JIMMY *climbs on top of Dale for a better angle to catch the chain,* CARI LEE *turns up the music enjoying all this.* JIMMY *pulls a chain out of* DALE's *mouth and struggles to yank the bounty from her brain.)*

KATE: *(Noting* DALE's *distress)* Jimmy?

JIMMY: It's stuck.

KATE: Stuck?

JIMMY: It's fine.

KATE: Is it stuck or is it fine?

CARI LEE: Just yank it!

JIMMY: It's a bit more delicate than that! You're doing good, Dale. Almost there. Almost got it. Hold tight. Here it comes!

(Finally, JIMMY liberates DALE's mortal clock and tugs it from her mouth. It's a beautiful pocket watch. ROWAN enters the shop. He carries a Ziploc bag filled with blood.)

ROWAN: Mr Wicker? *(To overcome the music)* Mr Wicker! *(He holds up the bag of blood.)* Here it is! The pocket watch. It's in there, swimming in the juice of itself. *(To JIMMY)* I know it looks bad. Looks worse than it is, probably. I didn't do much. Sprung a spring and the thing wouldn't stop leaking , but I wonder, Mr. Wicker, what did just happen in here? What's that you were doing to Dale, and you, Kate, holding her down with a strap, like? That looked strange and unpleasant.

CARI LEE: What did you do to my mortal clock?

ROWAN: Mortal clock?

CARI LEE: *WHAT DID YOU DO TO MY MORTAL CLOCK!*

ROWAN: I thought this was Dale's mother's pocket watch?

CARI LEE: I am Dale's mother.

ROWAN: How can that be? You're a young girl.

CARI LEE: My mortal clock.

ROWAN: I don't mean it as a slight, but a fact of chronology. I apologize. Your…mortal clock.

(ROWAN hands CARI LEE the bag. She hugs the blood filled bag, her poor little mortal clock.)

Scene 3
Busted Watches & Broken Hearts

(Later that evening. JIMMY *is at work on* CARI LEE's *mortal clock, fingers bloody. He has a white sheet spread out across his work area and it has become blood-spattered. She enters from upstairs. She has a mug of tea. She wanders around the shop.)*

JIMMY: Can't sleep?

CARI LEE: I dunno. I'm just up. I peeked into Dale's room. She's totally zonked. The way she's sleeping, like she fell out of an airplane and splatted on the pavement. Want some tea? Nerdface made it for me. I didn't ask for it. She's just like, here. Drink tea. Okay.

JIMMY: Kate's still up?

CARI LEE: Waiting for you.

Thanks for letting me stay here tonight.

JIMMY: Of course.

CARI LEE: No, really man, that's decent of you and Kate to let me stay. The pull-out couch is really comfortable. I got a pull-out couch at Scooter's place, but it's got springs stickin in my back and it's lumpy.

JIMMY: Who's this Scooter?

CARI LEE: He's kinda-sorta like my boyfriend in Seattle. Jealous?

JIMMY: Yeah I'm really jealous of a guy named Scooter.

CARI LEE: Scooter is too immature to be anything serious. I need someone who will fight for my honor and vanquish people who suck. Who will strangle a yak with his bare hands and bring me dinner. I need comfort in my life. I need a *man*. How's it going?

JIMMY: It's still bleeding.

CARI LEE: Can you fix it?

JIMMY: I can get the bleeding to stop.

CARI LEE: Can you *fix it* fix it?

(Pause)

JIMMY: I can't put any more time on it. You have only the time you had on it when it broke.

CARI LEE: *(Playful)* Oh yeah, who's the one that broke it? *(She looks at a wall marked with the yearly height of a growing child. She walks her fingers up the wall, up the years)* Dale stop growing after eleven years?

JIMMY: She stopped humoring me. Said she didn't want to see her age marked on a wall anymore.

(CARI LEE puts her back to the wall, measures her height with her hand to see how tall she is)

CARI LEE: Cari Lee. Seventeen years old.

JIMMY: You want to mark it?

CARI LEE: Nah. Don't need another reminder I'm not old enough to buy lotto tickets. And everybody gets older and older. I can't focus my eyes on anything. I can see fine but it's like there's nothing new to look at. Every day seems more washed out than the day before. I feel like a freak. You think that's what it was like for your mom too?

JIMMY: I don't know. I need to concentrate on this.

CARI LEE: Right.

JIMMY: You can keep talking, it's not bothering me.

CARI LEE: I thought about you and Dale every day. I sorta, like, kept track of things. If she'd be walking by this year, or talking by that year, and I always wanted to send her a card or something but I couldn't I don't know I got nervous and couldn't even get a stamp on the envelope. I kept picturing this version of myself who got older with you, who went to the park with you and taught my daughter how to ride a bicycle and then, one day, when she was old enough, we would enter a mother/daughter talent show like Marcia and Mrs Brady in that one episode of The Brady Bunch when they sang that song together dressed as hoboes.

(Pause)

JIMMY: I sometimes go to the lake.

CARI LEE: Elder Street beach?

JIMMY: Yeah. That crumbling concrete pier. And that night we sat there, y'know, when we were—when I was seventeen. We sat there with the picture from the first ultrasound we got earlier that day, when we found out it was a girl. And the moon was so full and bright, and we could see every detail. It was just me and you and this picture of our little girl. We sat there together and you held my hand and that was enough. That moment. I was so happy.

(CARI LEE massages JIMMY's neck.)

JIMMY: Cari Lee, what are you doing?

CARI LEE: I'm not doing anything. What, this doesn't feel good?

JIMMY: It feels okay, but...

CARI LEE: But what? *(Her massage becomes sensual. She swings onto his lap and kisses his neck his face,)* Touch me.

JIMMY: I can't.

CARI LEE: Touch me, Jimmy!

JIMMY: I don't want to get blood on your shirt.

(CARI LEE pulls her shirt off and places JIMMY's bloody hands on her body and she kisses him deeply.)

JIMMY: Cari Lee.

CARI LEE: Shut up.

(JIMMY *kisses* CARI LEE—*then stops.*)

CARI LEE: I love your scratchy stubble and your thinning hair and your smell, and you know what the problem was? You weren't *older* when you were younger. And now you're the most attractive wonderful thing and look at our daughter, man. It's made me so happy to see that you and Kate love her so much, and she's great and smart. I don't even know her, and she might be dead soon.

JIMMY: Don't say that.

CARI LEE: But I want something so incredible for you and Kate and Dale. Guess what I want.

JIMMY: I don't know.

CARI LEE: Guess!

JIMMY: I—a pony—I don't know.

CARI LEE: I wanna make a baby for you.

JIMMY: What?

CARI LEE: Gotta fix my mortal clock first. My body won't work right if you don't do that.

JIMMY: Wait. What?

CARI LEE: It isn't gonna be an accident this time. Let's do it right this time. Let's know what we want and let it happen.

JIMMY: You're serious.

CARI LEE: There's gonna be an empty space soon and you gotta fill it and helping you fill it is gonna fill me too. Start me up and I got just enough time to make a new life for you. Ten months, Jimmy. That's what's on my clock. It's just enough time.

(JIMMY *starts wiping his bloody handprints from* CARI LEE'*s skin, but gives her the towel to let her finish.*)

JIMMY: I've made a mess of you.

(JIMMY *hands* CARI LEE *her shirt. She pulls out* DALE'*s pocket watch and dangles it in front of him.*)

CARI LEE: Snuck into Dale's room while she was sleeping, stole it from her nightstand drawer.

JIMMY: Cari Lee, put it back. *(Pause)* Did you look at it?

CARI LEE: I thought we could look together. See how much time our daughter has left. It's important to see you only have so much time with her. You're blessed to know you can prepare yourself for such terrible emptiness.

(JIMMY *holds out his hands.* CARI LEE *drops* DALE'*s mortal clock into his hands. He rubs his thumb over the engraving…*)

JIMMY: *Dale… (He can't open it.)*

CARI LEE: Why don't you give me Dale's mortal clock.

JIMMY: I'm going to keep it safe and sound. Relax.

CARI LEE: I can't relax when I know we got different ideas of what safe and sound means. Give it to me.

JIMMY: No.

CARI LEE: What are you going to do with it?

JIMMY: If Dale is going to die soon, it's because I broke her seventeen years ago.

CARI LEE: We didn't know it would happen, Jimmy.

JIMMY: It's her life in my hand. It's so warm.

CARI LEE: Give it to me. Jimmy. I shouldn't have taken it from her.

(JIMMY *puts* DALE'*s pocket watch in his pocket.*)

CARI LEE: You know what you can do? You can fix my mortal clock and put it back the way it should be. That's what you can do. I'm done scamming the clockwork. I'm tired of being a freak. I want to be normal for the ten months I have and I want to do a good thing for once. You can fix what you broke. Now fix it. You can't leave me like this forever.

(JIMMY *goes to his work bench.*)

JIMMY: You ready to start growing up?

CARI LEE: Is anybody ever ready for that?

(JIMMY *fixes* CARI LEE's *mortal clock.*)

JIMMY: Feel anything?

CARI LEE: Every second.

(JIMMY *gives* CARI LEE *her bloody mortal clock swaddled in a towel.*)

(JIMMY *wipes the tears from* CARI LEE's *eyes, and the clocks in the shop tick tock and the sign in the window glows* WATCH & CLOCK REPAIR.)

END OF ACT ONE

ACT TWO

Scene 1
Helen & Her Most Unusual Pocket Watch

(It's 18 years earlier. Evening. RICHARD *[the actor who played* JIMMY *in ACT ONE] works on a clock at his workbench. His seventeen year old son* JIMMY *[the actor who played* ROWAN *in ACT TWO] sits on the bench outside the shop with a textbook in his lap, waiting.)*

HELEN: *(Offstage)* Richard?

RICHARD: Yes, dear? …Helen?

HELEN: *(Offstage)* Richard!

RICHARD: What!

HELEN: *(Offstage)* What do you mean what!

RICHARD: I mean "what" what. What!

HELEN: *(Offstage)* Come to bed!

RICHARD: Soon, I'll be up soon.

HELEN: *(Offstage)* "Soon, soon, soon."

RICHARD: One night, many years ago, there's a knock at this shop door. It was Helen. Under one arm she's lugging this big thick book and cradled in her other hand, a beautiful pocket watch. Broken. She says to my father, "Let me see your hands." He shows her his hands. And she looks at me and says, "Let me see your hands." She takes my little hands in hers, and she

asks my father if she can teach me a few things. Now,
yes, the majority of the business here is standard clock
repair and restoration. My father repaired watches and
clocks, my father's father repaired watches and clocks,
my father's father's fath—anyway, family occupation.
And this shop is a special place offering a special
service: mortal clock removal. Specializing in the poor
souls, the unfortunate few who, by fluke of nature
and genetics, wound up with a mortal clock where no
mortal clock should be: *(Taps his head)* Nestled snugly
in the brain where the tick tick tick of the slipping-
away life echoes from ear to ear. How do these people
find us? That's a mystery. I've asked and receive the
same answer from each. "Just a feeling," they say, "that
I could find help." Helen was the most special of all,
mortal clock removed and broken ages ago (she won't
tell me when as she claims she's forgotten). Well, my
father had never encountered a broken mortal clock
and was fascinated with her knowledge of mortal
clocks, and if she could teach us what she knew, she
was welcome to stay here as long as she needed. I got
older, ten, eleven, twelve…and Helen stayed the same.

*(HELEN [the actor who played KATE in ACT ONE] enters
from upstairs in her robe and slippers, looks to be in her 40s.
She has a drink in her hand, something boozy with ice. Her
hands shake and seem to be much older than the rest of her.)*

RICHARD: When I was twelve years old, I asked,
"Helen, why haven't we fixed your mortal clock?" And
she said

HELEN: Some things are worth waiting for.

RICHARD: Like what?

HELEN: Like a movie starring your favorite actress. Or
a full moon over the lake. Or waiting for a person who
you know you're meant to love but isn't quite ready to

love you back. (*She returns to her drink. She exits outside the shop for some fresh air.*)

RICHARD: She would never let me peek at her mortal clock. She kept me blindfolded as I learned my craft. And she said, "One day, your age will catch up to mine. That's the day you will fix my pocket watch." … and so I grew older. Helen stayed the same. My father died "too soon" as we say of untimely deaths due to bad habits. And maybe by now it's clear that this once immortal woman is now mortal and she is my wife. I fixed her mortal clock. I gave her mortality so we could be together, age together, have a child together.

JIMMY: Hi mom.

HELEN: Jimmy sweetheart. What are you doing out here this late?

JIMMY: Waiting.

HELEN: Ahhhh, yes. Waiting. For that girl, I suppose.

(HELEN *drinks, looks at the sky.* RICHARD *dangles her pocket watch.*)

RICHARD: This is Helen's mortal clock. I swore that I would never ever look at the time of her death. I kept my promise. Until this evening, after I found…this. (*He gets a shoebox.*)

JIMMY: Mom? …What are you looking at?

HELEN: I remember when you could see the stars, but now the lights from the city flood the sky.

RICHARD: What if…what if the person who you know you're meant to love isn't enough to make the years worthwhile? (*He takes a handgun out of the shoebox.*) I now know when my wife is going to die. (*He puts the handgun back in the shoebox and puts it away.*)

HELEN: Goodnight, sweetheart.

JIMMY: 'Night, Mom.

(HELEN *enters the shop.*)

HELEN: Come to bed, Richard.

RICHARD: I'll be there soon.

HELEN: Soon.

(HELEN *takes off her slippers and throws them at* RICHARD.)

RICHARD: Your slippers have fallen off again, Helen.

HELEN: Do you know what clock I need?

RICHARD: Mm, what clock do you need.

HELEN: The one set on Richard-Time. Half past eventually. Quarter 'til soon. Make me that clock with those words, so I know when you're coming to bed.

RICHARD: Why?

HELEN: You wake me when you climb into bed, that's why.

RICHARD: Do I?

HELEN: You know this.

RICHARD: I do?

HELEN: Wasn't it just the other night you cannon-balled onto your side of the bed. And wasn't I nearly concussed on the nightstand, sprung off my side of the bed.

RICHARD: You exaggerate to the point of indecency.

HELEN: Learn to set gently on your side. If not for me, then for your next wife. She'll appreciate the courtesy.

(RICHARD *looks at* HELEN; *a beat. He busies himself with his work again.*)

RICHARD: You assume I'd remarry.

HELEN: Wouldn't you? That leggy blonde creature in those tacky pumps.

RICHARD: I don't know who you're talking about.

HELEN: Body tight as a rubber band, likes to *browse?*

RICHARD: She's married anyway, and—

HELEN: Ohh you've checked her availability.

RICHARD: Married, says the rock on her finger, and besides, she lives in *Kenilworth.* You're giving my pocket book much too much credit to attract such a woman. *(He begins putting things away.)* I'll be up now.

HELEN: Did *now* just fall from your lips?

RICHARD: *Now* is my gift to you, Helen.

(Outside the shop, CARI LEE enters. She's eight months pregnant.)

CARI LEE: Whatup bastard!

JIMMY: Whatup yourself, fatty.

CARI LEE: *(Shouts through the shop window)* Hi Mr and Mrs Wicker!!! I'm doing great, thanks for asking!!!

HELEN: There she is, the little hellion.

RICHARD: Look on the bright side.

HELEN: The bright side, the bright side, the side that is bright—remind me—which side would that be?

RICHARD: We'll be grandparents. Isn't that right, Grandma?

HELEN: Mmgreat. *(Drinks)*

CARI LEE: I'm constipated. This is like part baby, part elephant turd. Swear to god. I walk into The Bean Counter. Guess what. Bathroom is for customers only and they won't give me the key on the stupid paddle. Like, on principle, I'm not gonna drop a buck on crappy French roast so I can use their bathroom to pop a dookie. I got boundaries.

JIMMY: You have boundaries?

(RICHARD has become distracted by his work again)

HELEN: *Richard?*

RICHARD: *What?!*

HELEN: Come to bed.

RICHARD: In a minute, Helen. *(He puts a cigarette in his mouth.)*

HELEN: Those are going to kill you. If not by black of lung then by stray butt igniting your pants. It's a terrible vice.

RICHARD: A vice for a vice, dear:

(RICHARD *drops his cigarette in* HELEN's *drink. She dumps her ruined drink in his lap. She will exit and get more slippers and throw them at him.)*

JIMMY: Did you study at all today?

CARI LEE: You ever see the movie *On the Waterfront?*—

JIMMY: You didn't study.

CARI LEE: *(Continuous)* —I rented it. Black and white movie, right. Marlon Brando, right, and he's totally hot. I'd do him. If I had a time machine I'd fly back to 1954 and do Brando. I'd do him in the back seat of my time machine.

JIMMY: You didn't bring your textbook.

CARI LEE: Who would you do?

JIMMY: You're going to fail Spanish.

CARI LEE: Sooooo, who would you do?

JIMMY: I don't know. Your mom.

CARI LEE: Have you *seen* my mom? She's a total dog.

JIMMY: She's kinda pretty.

CARI LEE: She's a droopy faced booze hound, but do whoever you want. You do my mom, I'll do your dad. I bet he was a cutie when he was seventeen.

(Looking at RICHARD *and* HELEN *throwing slippers:)*

CARI LEE: Old people in love are so weird.

JIMMY: They're not in love. She says, "you know what I *don't* want for my birthday this year? You know what I *don't* want? Slippers. I don't want slippers. Do not buy me slippers." And he buys her slippers! Every year. Gets them gift wrapped at Marshall Fields. The same slippers. Same brand. Same style. Same color.

*(*HELEN *runs out of slippers.)*

HELEN: Goodnight Richard. See you tomorrow. *(She exits.)*

*(*RICHARD *picks up slippers.)*

CARI LEE: Why do you think he gets her slippers every year?

JIMMY: Because he's stupid.

CARI LEE: Forget the Spanish, man, you need a little schoolin in the ways of the elder species. He *likes* a little slipper slappin. *(Gestures ass-slapping)* You see my drift? You catchin it? Think about it.

*(*RICHARD *opens the shop door with an armful of slippers.)*

RICHARD: Not too late.

JIMMY: All right, dad.

CARI LEE: Hey, Mr Wicker, how's it shakin. Slippers, huh?

RICHARD: Slippers? Slippers, yes, slippers. Yes. I'm going to bed, Jimmy. Lock up when you come in, okay?

JIMMY: Sure, Dad.

CARI LEE: G'night, Mr Wicker!

RICHARD: Goodnight, Cari Lee. *(He exits.)*

CARI LEE: See?

JIMMY: See *what*?

CARI LEE: Your parents are gonna have wild monkey sex tonight.

(JIMMY *slams his textbook shut.*)

CARI LEE: What?

JIMMY: You wasted my time.

CARI LEE: I wasted your time.

JIMMY: You were an hour late, Cari Lee. I waited for you, and you wasted my time.

CARI LEE: Jimmybear.

JIMMY: Forget it. No, forget it. We're gonna sit here. And you're gonna talk about whatever movie you watched today, and I'll be like "we gotta study" and you'll be like "visualize your parents having sex" and you know what? You know what?

(CARI LEE *kisses* JIMMY *deeply. The textbook is easily discarded. He puts his hand on her breast. She moves it off. He puts his hand on it again. She moves it off again.*)

JIMMY: I wanna touch your tits.

CARI LEE: No.

JIMMY: May I touch your tits please?

CARI LEE: No. Okay fine.

JIMMY: They got bigger.

CARI LEE: I'm pregnant, moron, that's what happens. Hey—easy—my boobs hurt.

JIMMY: They're nice. I really like them.

CARI LEE: All right. That's enough. Stop. I'm done. Jimmy, I said stop, all right?

(JIMMY *stops.* CARI LEE *and* JIMMY *sit quietly for a moment. She lets him touch her belly, lean down, listen.*)

JIMMY: I heard something! What was that? I heard something.

CARI LEE: I farted.

JIMMY: Oh.

CARI LEE: Just wait. She'll move.

JIMMY: *(Waits, feels something)* Whoa. Weird.

CARI LEE: Yeah. Weird.

JIMMY: Pretty soon, huh. Are you excited? I'm excited.

CARI LEE: I'm glad you're excited.

JIMMY: Have you been taking all your vitamins and drinking milk and stuff like that.

CARI LEE: Yeah, yeah.

JIMMY: *Have you?*

CARI LEE: *Yes.* God. Shut up. *(She stands.)*

JIMMY: Where are you going?

CARI LEE: I saw something in the alley I wanna get. Something special just for you, Jimmybear.

(JIMMY stands, goes in the shop, turns on some more lights. CARI LEE exits and returns carrying the coat rack)

JIMMY: What is that?

CARI LEE: Coat rack.

JIMMY: Thanks for bringing in garbage from the alley, that's great.

CARI LEE: What're you talking about "garbage," it's a really excellent coat rack. Man, you don't appreciate me. That's what our life together would be like. Me bringing you garbage and you being like "that's garbage." *(She will find* RICHARD's *pack of cigarettes. She will light one and smoke.)* You like fixing this stuff? Clocks and watches n stuff. Is this what you're going to do with your life?

JIMMY: Well this stuff, and mortal clocks. Helping people who have it in their heads. "The unfortunate few," my dad says, all serious. I don't think it's that unfortunate because it's how I met you, and—*are you smoking*?!

CARI LEE: No. Just this one.

JIMMY: You're pregnant, Cari Lee!

CARI LEE: What? I am? *(Looks down)* Oh my god!

JIMMY: Put it out.

CARI LEE: Hey. Man. I'm stressed out like you have no idea.

(JIMMY *will try taking the cigarette away from* CARI LEE *and she slaps him away*)

JIMMY: You can't keep doing stupid stuff.

CARI LEE: I don't do stupid stuff.

JIMMY: You're smoking a cigarette!

CARI LEE: It's *one* cigarette.

(JIMMY *will grab* CARI LEE'S *wrist to disarm her of the cigarette.*)

CARI LEE: Hey—ow—I'm *fragile*!

JIMMY: You got a baby to think of. Stop being selfish.

CARI LEE: Well, I am selfish. Selfish is my thing. I'm not changing anytime soon, not for you, not for anybody.

JIMMY: Y'know what? Grow up.

CARI LEE: Y'know what? *(Gives him the finger:)* Sit on it and spin.

(Pause)

JIMMY: I think we should get married. I'm serious.

CARI LEE: You're not serious, you're antique. You're more antique than the clocks your dad fixes. So you knocked me up, Jimmybear, big deal, don't need to get all shotgun wedding about it.

JIMMY: I want to see you more. I want to take care of you. I want to know things.

CARI LEE: Well, next time I fart, I'll let you know. I'll call you up, how bout that? I'll be all like *(Punching numbers on an imaginary phone) beep-boop-boop beep-boop-beep-beep,* "Hey Jimmy, guess what? I farted." Where do you want this? *(The coat rack. She has to sit down.)*

JIMMY: Are you all right?

CARI LEE: Fine. ...I heard a rumor today. I heard Nerdface has the hots for you. She wants to, like, jump your bones.

JIMMY: Don't call her Nerdface, she doesn't like being called Nerdface.

CARI LEE: Oh, so you do like her.

JIMMY: I'm just saying don't call her Nerdface.

CARI LEE: If you like her so much why don't you ask *her* to marry you.

JIMMY: I don't like Nerdface! —Kate, I mean—and what's your problem, why'd you graffiti that word on her locker?

CARI LEE: I dunno, I just did.

JIMMY: Yeah, look who's jealous now.

CARI LEE: I'm not jealous! So what if Nerdface likes you. I don't care.

JIMMY: I want to marry you, Cari Lee. I haven't been more sure of anything in my life as I'm sure of that. I love you.

CARI LEE: Whatever.

(JIMMY holds up CARI LEE's mortal clock.)

CARI LEE: Where'd—hey!

JIMMY: My mom and dad said you gotta keep it safe and sound. Does this look very safe and sound?

CARI LEE: It *was* safe and sound.

JIMMY: Then how come it's in my hand?

CARI LEE: You stole it off me while you were feeling me up, you jerk. Give it back.

JIMMY: Can I have a kiss first?

CARI LEE: If I wanted to kiss an asshole, I'd ask you to bend over.

(CARI LEE *reaches for her mortal clock.* JIMMY *pulls it out of her reach.*)

JIMMY: What if I looked at your time?

CARI LEE: It's not for you to see.

JIMMY: It's in my hands, I can do whatever I want with it. Maybe it would teach you to be not so careless with important things.

CARI LEE: Give it back.

JIMMY: Tell me when you're going to die. *(Pause)* I love you, Cari Lee.

CARI LEE: Don't say that. It's a stupid thing to say to someone. I want my mortal clock back. Just…give it back, man. Okay? Give it back. Give it back, Jimmy. *(Crying now)* Give it back. Is this what you want, you wanna see me cry, you wanna teach me a lesson and make me cry? You want tears? Here:

(CARI LEE *wipes her cheek, and slaps* JIMMY *across the face with her wet hand.*)

JIMMY: I love you!

CARI LEE: Jimmy, goddammit, give me my mortal clock!!! *(She has a labor pain.)* Ohh!

JIMMY: Are you okay? Cari Lee?

CARI LEE: Mm.

JIMMY: Cari Lee...

CARI LEE: Hm.

JIMMY: Is it the baby, is the baby coming, is this it?

(Another pain)

JIMMY: We gotta go to the hospital.

CARI LEE: I guess I shoulda said goodbye sooner than this.

JIMMY: What? No. No goodbye. You're having a baby not saying goodbye.

CARI LEE: I'm sorry, Jimmy.

JIMMY: You're not dying this isn't time to say goodbye. Is it? Cari Lee? Is it... *(Pause. He opens the watch to look at her time.)* No. Oh god no. *(He takes her pocket watch to his dad's workbench)*

CARI LEE: It's all right Jimmy. I lived my whole life knowing. It's no big deal.

JIMMY: Screw this. I'm putting more time on your mortal clock.

CARI LEE: Your mom and dad said it doesn't work like that.

JIMMY: It's a mechanical thing.

CARI LEE: Yeah, but it came outta my *head*.

JIMMY: Mom and Dad think rules can't be bent or broken and they certainly wouldn't *try*. It can't hurt anything to try. We're gonna have a baby and you're going to be there for her. You're not going to die tonight. I won't let it happen.

(JIMMY opens the back of the pocket watch. CARI LEE gasps, struck dizzy.)

CARI LEE: I dunno Jimmy, I dunno this is such a hot idea. Do you know what you're doing?

JIMMY: I know what I'm doing. I've fixed pocket watches before.

CARI LEE: *Pocket watches*, not mortal clocks.

JIMMY: Do you want to die tonight?

(Pause)

CARI LEE: Hurry up and do it.

(JIMMY *sticks a tool into the watch and twists. Blood spurts and oozes. He cranks the watch. There's a horrible terrible wretched ratcheting noise.* CARI LEE *reacts to each crank of her mortal clock.)*

JIMMY: Oh my god. It's working. It's working! I added a whole month to your life!

(JIMMY *does it again. Another terrible ratcheting noise)*

CARI LEE: Ahhhhgod.

(JIMMY *ratchets the watch again.)*

JIMMY: Another month!

CARI LEE: It's working??

(JIMMY *ratchets the watch.)*

JIMMY: Three months. *(He ratchets the watch.)* Four!

CARI LEE: Jimmy.

JIMMY: Five!

CARI LEE: Jimmy.

JIMMY: Six!

CARI LEE: Something's wrong.

JIMMY: Seven!

CARI LEE: Something's very very wrong. You shouldn't do this.

JIMMY: Eight!

CARI LEE: Jimmy stop.

JIMMY: Nine!

CARI LEE: Stop!

JIMMY: Ten!

CARI LEE: STOOOOOOOOOOOP!!!!! *(Silence)* You did something to the baby.

(RICHARD and HELEN enter from upstairs. They see the blood on JIMMY's hands.)

HELEN: What did you do, Jimmy?

JIMMY: I...I gave Cari Lee more time. Ten months.

RICHARD: That's not possible. Give me that.

(RICHARD takes CARI LEE's pocket watch from JIMMY. HELEN attends to CARI LEE.)

HELEN: How do you feel?

CARI LEE: Dizzy.

RICHARD: Helen, it's broken.

CARI LEE: What happened to me?

HELEN: Ssshhhh. Richard, what looks broken?

RICHARD: Maybe it's the center wheel or maybe it's the regulator. Blood's clotting around both.

CARI LEE: I feel strange.

HELEN: Follow my finger with your eyes. *(She passes her finger back and forth in front of CARI LEE's face.)* Hmm. *(She places her hand on CARI LEE's forehead and listens to her back.)*

CARI LEE: What's she doing?

(HELEN gives CARI LEE a little slap on the back)

CARI LEE: Ah! What the heck?

HELEN: You're stopped.

CARI LEE: Stopped?

HELEN: Your mortal clock is no longer ticking and you are no longer aging. There is extra time on here, but until the mortal clock is fixed you are stopped.

CARI LEE: What about the baby?

HELEN: Her mortal clock won't start until the moment she's born, and she won't be born until this is fixed. There's still tension in the spring, so that's good.

CARI LEE: What are you saying?

HELEN: Your pregnancy may last a bit longer than the usual nine months.

RICHARD: But, Helen. It's not possible to add more time to a mortal clock. Right? It's not possible. Helen? Helen?

HELEN: You said you gave her ten months, Jimmy?

JIMMY: Yeah, ten months, that's all.

(HELEN *consults her big book of mortal clockery.* RICHARD *and* HELEN *aside, but certainly* JIMMY *overhears some of this*)

RICHARD: Is there something you haven't told me?

HELEN: Time can be stolen from a tethered mortal clock.

RICHARD: Well *that* would have been good know!

(HELEN *works out some calculations, pencil on paper…*)

HELEN: It takes an exponential amount of energy to siphon off another mortal clock.

Ten months added to Cari Lee's mortal clock could very well be *years* taken from the baby … with the rate of transfer….(*She puts down the pencil…*) Oh dear.

JIMMY: Cari Lee…

CARI LEE: Don't touch me, Jimmy.

JIMMY: But you would have been dead tonight!

CARI LEE: I said don't touch me, don't break me anymore.

RICHARD: Is this rate of transfer absolute? Did you do your calculations correctly?

HELEN: "Did I do my calculations correctly" *of course* I did them correctly.

RICHARD: May I look? How much time was stolen from the baby.

(HELEN *crumples the paper.*)

RICHARD: Since I was a little boy, you swore to me that time could not be added, subtracted, or otherwise changed.

HELEN: A mother and child are tethered until the child is born, that is the one and only exception.

RICHARD: Do you swear?

HELEN: *(Hesitating, slightly)* I swear.

(A moment)

RICHARD: You don't know anything for sure, do you?

HELEN: How dare you say that, Richard.

RICHARD: Maybe it's about time I say it.

HELEN: Give me Cari Lee's mortal clock.

RICHARD: No.

HELEN: Give it here, Richard.

RICHARD: No.

HELEN: Richard!

RICHARD: I'll figure it out.

HELEN: There's nothing for you to figure out!

RICHARD: Helen, no!

(In the tussle for CARI LEE's *pocket watch, it slips from* RICHARD's *hands and drops. Her labor pains resume and she cries out.)*

HELEN: What just happened?

RICHARD: You dropped her mortal clock!

HELEN: I didn't drop it! *You* dropped it.

RICHARD: I wouldn't have dropped it if you hadn't've—

JIMMY: WOULD SOMEBODY DO *SOMETHING*?! *(To* CARI LEE*)* It's gonna be all right. You're doing great!

CARI LEE: Shut up!

JIMMY: God, I love you so much.

RICHARD: *(Retrieving* CARI LEE's *pocket watch)* It's running! I don't understand how it's running.

HELEN: That spring isn't going to stay taut much longer. But maybe it'll run just long enough to deliver this baby before it stops for good.

RICHARD: I'll call the hospital.

HELEN: Pffft! No time for that. Jimmy, go upstairs and get some warm water and clean towels.

RICHARD: Here? On my floor?

HELEN: I'm afraid you don't have much choice in the matter. Jimmy go.

RICHARD: She can't have a baby on the floor, I just cleaned the floor.

HELEN: Tend to her mortal clock, make sure the blood doesn't clot around that spring. I'll tend to everything else.

JIMMY: Oh my god this is awesome.

HELEN: Jimmy!—how many times do I have to tell you? Now!

(JIMMY *runs upstairs.*)

CARI LEE: Are you sure you know what you're doing, Mrs. Wicker?

HELEN: Oh yes. I worked quite a few years as a midwife in the 1840s and 50s.

CARI LEE: The 18whatnow? (*A sharp pain*) Ohh I feel sick I'm gonna pass out.

HELEN: Take my hand. There. There. Breathe. Good. You're all right. Now Richard's there tending your mortal clock and Jimmy will be down again soon to help.

CARI LEE: I can't do this.

HELEN: You can do this, Cari Lee. I know you can. And, think, soon this will be another memory and you'll have a little baby girl for all your trouble tonight.

(CARI LEE *howls. Blackout*)

Scene 2
The Shoebox & The Chain-Snagged Heart

(*Afternoon.* RICHARD *is working. He is not feeling well. The phone rings. He answers.*)

RICHARD: Wicker's Watch and Clock Repair, this is Richard.
*

Hello, Mrs Herman.
*

I'm sorry, the parts aren't in yet.
*

Germany, it's a German watch. I'll give you a ring

when I get those parts. Thanks for being patient. Bye now. *(Hangs up)*

(RICHARD *returns to his work.* HELEN *enters, drink in hand. She watches him. He is aware of her lurking.)*

RICHARD: What?

HELEN: Is that Cari Lee's mortal clock you are working on?

RICHARD: No.

HELEN: Why not?

RICHARD: It's very complicated. And I have a lot of work to do, Helen. Business in this shop hasn't stopped.

HELEN: Ahh, but Cari Lee's mortal clock has stopped. It has been stopped for three weeks.

RICHARD: I told you, I will get to it.

HELEN: Priorities, Richard: her mortal clock must be fixed. The girl can't remain a record spinning on the table without the needle down. The music must play, a life must continue toward its final notes.

RICHARD: If she needs to be repaired immediately, maybe you should repair her yourself.

HELEN: My hands are useless. You know that.

RICHARD: They don't shake so when you concentrate.

HELEN: Those times are few and far between.

RICHARD: I've seen them steady.

HELEN: I can't remember when that would be.

RICHARD: When Jimmy was a little boy and you'd tie his shoes.

HELEN: Mortal clocks are not shoelaces. My hands cannot repair mortal clocks. I demand you repair Cari Lee's mortal clock.

RICHARD: If I repair her mortal clock, she will be dead in ten months.

HELEN: Yes.

RICHARD: If I repair her clock...I will be killing her.

HELEN: Your work is not a moral decision, Richard. Your responsibility is to repair flawed mechanics. It is your job and it is your duty. Go get her mortal clock. Let's begin.

(RICHARD obeys, gets CARI LEE's mortal clock. HELEN makes sure he sits at his workbench and sets out her book for him to consult.)

HELEN: Do you need the blindfold? Would that help?

RICHARD: Yes.

(HELEN gets a blindfold. She ties it over RICHARD's eyes.)

HELEN: Why didn't you come to bed last night?

RICHARD: I was busy.

HELEN: Busy doing what?

RICHARD: If you were that interested, you should've come down to see for yourself. *(He wipes his brow.)*

HELEN: What's wrong?

RICHARD: Nothing.

HELEN: Richard.

RICHARD: I'm tired. I feel feverish when I don't sleep.

HELEN: You'll have a nap later.

RICHARD: Helen?

HELEN: Yes.

RICHARD: If life is so absolute, so finite, so pre-determined, so controlled, so fated. If that is so, then how come Jimmy took this very mortal clock and added ten months to Cari Lee's life?

HELEN: That time was stolen from her baby, it was special circumstances, a mother and a child--

RICHARD: Tethered mortal clocks, you've said. But I don't think those special circumstances were so special.

(HELEN *laughs.*)

RICHARD: Don't laugh at me.

HELEN: I'm sorry, I don't mean to laugh. It's a physical bond, Richard. The mortal clock in the child is born from the mortal clock of the mother.

RICHARD: But, listen, okay? Listen: what if it could be forged between any two mortal clocks? And they could be connected. What if that were possible?

HELEN: Richard. You need your nap now.

RICHARD: Don't treat me like a child, Helen.

HELEN: Please, take a break from this work and go take a nap.

(RICHARD *takes off the blindfold.*)

RICHARD: How can I sleep when I know that today is the last day of your life?

(*Pause*)

HELEN: You... You promised me you wouldn't look.

RICHARD: I had to look.

HELEN: You should never have looked at the time on my mortal clock.

RICHARD: Well you shouldn't have left it rattling around your nightstand drawer. Didn't I say it's like leaving a cupcake on the table and telling the fat kid not to eat it?

HELEN: You said you would never be the fat kid.

RICHARD: Well I am the fat kid! What do fat kids do?
They eat cupcakes. Fat kids like cupcakes, if you leave
a cupcake on the table, Helen, the fat kid will *eat it!*

HELEN: You swore you would never look at the time on
my mortal clock!

RICHARD: And you swore time was absolute!

HELEN: It is absolute!

(RICHARD *takes out a shoebox and places it on the counter.*)

RICHARD: Do you want to explain this to me?

HELEN: No.

RICHARD: Is this your intent?

HELEN: Put it away.

RICHARD: IS THIS YOUR INTENT, HELEN?!

HELEN: Put it away, Richard. Jimmy is coming.

(RICHARD *puts the shoebox aside.* JIMMY *enters from
outside.*)

JIMMY: I'm not here. Tell her I'm sick, like, throw-up
sick. I may have to climb out the upstairs window if
she doesn't go away.

(*Outside,* KATE *[the actor who played* DALE *in ACT ONE]
enters. She wears a cheerleading uniform, tight aggressive
hair pulled back with a scrunchie, and thick glasses. She's,
like, totally pissed.* JIMMY *exits upstairs.* KATE *enters the
shop.*)

KATE: Hello Mr and Mrs Wicker. How are you? Is
Jimmy home?

HELEN: What did he do?

KATE: I have a list of grievances actually, but
specifically, it's more like what *didn't* Jimmy do.
Jimmy *promised* he'd do his half of the final project
for European History, and I gave him a choice—I

said, "Jimmy, which part of this project would you
rather be responsible for? The paper or the in-class
presentation." And he said the presentation, and I
would do the eight page paper. And I've been calling
him every other day, as you know because you answer
the phone, asking "how's it going, Jimmy" to which he
always responds, "it's going quite well, Kate, thanks."
Today was our turn to do our presentation in class.
Jimmy. Didn't. Prepare. Anything. We got a C. I do not
get Cs.

HELEN: JIMMY!

JIMMY: *(Offstage)* I'm really really sick, can you tell
her to come back tomorrow when I'm not so horribly
contagious?

RICHARD: Jimmy! Get down here!

(JIMMY enters.)

JIMMY: Oh, hi, Kate. How are you? You look really nice
today. Did you do something different with your…
uniform?

KATE: I am waitlisted at HARVARD! Do you
UNDERSTAND what that means?! That MEANS I
can't get anything less than an A in European History
this semester if they're going to ACCEPT ME, which
they're NOT, because OUR PROJECT TOGETHER is
going to drag my final grade down to a B!

RICHARD: A "B" is above average, isn't it?

(HELEN shushes RICHARD.)

JIMMY: Yeeeeah. I'm really sorry about that?

KATE: Is that a question? Are you asking me if you're
really sorry about that?

JIMMY: No, I'm really sorry.

KATE: You could've *told* me you weren't going to do it.

JIMMY: I didn't want you to get angry.

KATE: Ohhh, you think this is my happy face. This
is not my happy face. My happy face looks like this:
(Makes a scary happy face) Just so you're not *confused*
next time. Oh. *Oh!* *(Leans head back, pinches nose)* I need
a Kleenex! I need a Kleenex!

(JIMMY hands KATE a Kleenex. She squeezes her nose.)

KATE: Yes, perfect, this is perfect, this is just *sooo* what
I needed right now. My day is now complete. I can't
wait to go to a state school.

JIMMY: *Kate.*

KATE: Leave me alone, I'm hemorrhaging out my face.

(JIMMY grabs KATE's arm.)

KATE: Don't *touch me* Jimmy!

JIMMY: Wow—geez—sorry. I, Kate, I'm sorry, I got
other things, you know, on my mind. I can't do
everything. I'm sorry, I'm sorry, a thousand times I'm
sorry!

KATE: I don't care if you have more saris than the entire
country of India, you shouldn't've promised me you
were going to do something when you totally knew
you weren't. If you had told me you weren't going to
bother doing it, I would've done it.

JIMMY: Kate, I got other things, I have a baby now.

KATE: Oh yeah, where is she, is she *invisible?*

JIMMY: She's with Cari Lee.

KATE: And where's Cari Lee, is *she* invisible?

JIMMY: I don't know where Cari Lee is! I don't know!
She left and didn't tell me where she was going or
when she'll be back and I don't know where Cari Lee
and my daughter are! Okay???

(Beat)

KATE: I know you got other things going on right now. I would've picked up the slack for you if you needed some help. I would've done that for you. I realize that. I didn't mean to make you upset.

JIMMY: I'm not upset. I'm not upset.

HELEN: Where are you going, Jimmy.

JIMMY: I DON'T KNOW! *(He exits.)*

KATE: I apologize for yelling in your shop, Mr and Mrs Wicker.

HELEN: It's all right, Kate. Thank you for wanting him to do well.

(KATE exits the shop. CARI LEE enters with the baby.)

CARI LEE: Hi.

KATE: Hi. Jimmy's really upset.

CARI LEE: What did you do?

KATE: Y'know what, I just really do not feel like talking to you, Cari Lee.

CARI LEE: Fine. Don't.

KATE: *(Looks at the baby)* She's cute.

CARI LEE: You want her?

KATE: What?

CARI LEE: Joke. *(She enters the shop with the baby.)*

HELEN: Hello Cari Lee.

RICHARD: Where have you been?

CARI LEE: I've been around.

RICHARD: We've been worried about you.

HELEN: How is everything?

CARI LEE: Good. I guess.

HELEN: Is she eating all right?

CARI LEE: Yeah, she sucks tit like a champ, so obviously she's Jimmy's daughter.

HELEN: Well I could use a drink. *(She exits to pour a drink.)*

CARI LEE: Did you fix my mortal clock yet, Mr Wicker?

RICHARD: It's getting close.

CARI LEE: How close?

RICHARD: Close.

(RICHARD looks at the baby. CARI LEE ambles about. She will open up the shoebox)

RICHARD: She's going to be smart, I can tell, the way she's taking the whole world in with her eyes.

CARI LEE: But she's gonna be dead soon. Right? I stole her time. I know that's where my extra time came from. Well I don't want it. It's hers. Can't you put it back on her clock?

RICHARD: What did you say?

CARI LEE: Can't you just, like, put it back?

(RICHARD thinks about that—he goes to the big book. CARI LEE looks at the shoebox. Opens it. She picks the handgun out of the shoebox. She puts the gun to her head.)

CARI LEE: You ever just wanna test these mortal clocks?

(RICHARD looks up to see CARI LEE with the gun.)

CARI LEE: Don't you ever wonder?

RICHARD: Give me the gun.

CARI LEE: Like, what if you're supposed to die in your sleep when you're eighty but then one morning in your thirties you wake up and say, screw it, blammo splat brains everywhere. What if I pulled the trigger. What if I just did that.

RICHARD: Cari Lee.

(RICHARD *holds out his hand.* CARI LEE *gives the gun to him. He puts it away.*)

CARI LEE: Don't I have any say in this? I mean, I've never been punctual for anything in my entire life! Do I really gotta die when a stupid clock says I'm gonna die?

(RICHARD *clutches his chest pained*)

CARI LEE: Mr Wicker? You okay?

(RICHARD *nods, still pained.* HELEN *enters with a drink and the bottle.*)

HELEN: Richard.
Are you having a heart attack?

RICHARD: I'm fine.

HELEN: You don't look it.

RICHARD: *I'm fine.* (*He returns the gun to the shoebox.*)

CARI LEE: Maybe I should leave.

HELEN: Maybe you should.

RICHARD: Stay.

HELEN: Richard.

RICHARD: Stay. Please. You need to stay. I have your mortal clock here, and you need to stay for it.

(RICHARD's *immediate pain will subside, but he will continue to perspire and deteriorate and ache throughout the scene.* HELEN *will continue to drink.*)

HELEN: (*She opens her pocket watch to show him*) Richard. I have known since I was a little girl that today was my day, this hour my hour. My mortal clocks says this is my deadline. I have always been punctual.
Do you see? What does it say? You've looked at my mortal clock. Richard what does it say? It's never wrong.

RICHARD: By your own hand?

HELEN: What catastrophe could befall me other than myself? I'm not sick, I'm not leaving this shop to be hit by a car or have a piano dropped on my head, and I have always known that my time would end by my own hand. All I want to do is take my shoebox, have one more drink, wash my feet, and that'll be that.

RICHARD: That'll be that.

HELEN: Yes.

RICHARD: When did you decide this.

HELEN: Richard, mortal clocks are never wrong.

RICHARD: What if they are. What if your mortal clock is wrong.

(HELEN *goes for the gun in the shoebox.* RICHARD *doesn't let her have it.*)

RICHARD: Helen. Say: I will not kill myself.

HELEN: I will not kill myself. Now give me my shoebox.

RICHARD: Why do you have to kill yourself? You don't have to do it! See? Instead of killing yourself you could NOT kill yourself.

HELEN: But I have to.

RICHARD: But you don't!

HELEN: You're still the stupid boy you've always been, Richard.

RICHARD: You didn't think me stupid when I was a boy. You loved me once. What you said to me, I remember, a few weeks back. How I should learn to set gently in bed for my next wife... do you remember saying that to me?

HELEN: Yes. I remember.

RICHARD: I'm not going to remarry.

HELEN: Richard. I want you to be happy.

RICHARD: Another woman won't make me happy.

HELEN: But you should be happy with *somebody*.

RICHARD: I am happy with somebody. I'm happy with you.

HELEN: Please stop lying.

RICHARD: I'm not.

HELEN: STOP LYING TO ME!

RICHARD: You loved me once.

HELEN: Stop.

RICHARD: *(To* CARI LEE*)* She did. She loved me once. She loved my hands. These hands that could repair her mortal clock. I was a boy. A young boy. How old do you think Helen is?

CARI LEE: I, uh. I dunno.

HELEN: What difference would it make, Richard, how old I am.

RICHARD: Or what was that you told me when I was a boy? What did you say to me? What did you say to me when I was a seven year old boy and you were a grown woman.

(Pause)

HELEN: The question is not how old I am. But when was I born.

RICHARD: When were you born, Helen?

HELEN: I was born the minute I touched your hands, Richard. I used to believe that the man who would fix my mortal clock would also fix me and I would be content. Richard, you're a loyal man, loyal to a fault, but I won't have you lying to my face saying you're *happy*. That you've *always been* happy?

RICHARD: But it's true.

HELEN: You're saying it because I'm going to be dead soon.

RICHARD: I'm saying it because it's the truth.

HELEN: To say you're happy *can't* be the truth. It can't be. When you've been so unhappy with me and I have been equally unhappy with you! I've been unhappy and I won't go to my grave feeling that I've missed being happy because I didn't know what I was looking for. This can't be the happiest two people can ever be. *(She tries to get her shoebox.)*

RICHARD: Can I tell you the only wish I have? My only wish, Helen, is that I had looked at your mortal clock sooner. All the things I would have done differently. Knowing now I should have savored the years with you, sweetly on my tongue. What can I say to you other than please don't do this. Is there anything I can say to change this? Helen, I love you.

(Pause)

HELEN: How dare you be so selfish.

RICHARD: Me selfish!?

HELEN: Yes!

RICHARD: You're the one about to put a bullet in yourself and it's *me selfish!*

HELEN: Richard. That was the most terrible thing you could say to me right now. I was prepared to go. And now… you've unhinged me. The universe has no respect for love or family or feeling. It exists and it's big and it's empty and now it is time for me to go. Everybody has their time. Don't fight it, Cari Lee. Just go. Go.

(RICHARD *cries in pain, clutching his chest.* HELEN *goes to him.)*

HELEN: Ohh Richard. What's happening to you?

(CARI LEE *exits the shop with the baby.)*

KATE: Are you okay?

CARI LEE: *(Machine-gun urgency)* Would you tell Jimmy I say bye? Like I'm sorry I had to run, but that's the way it's gonna be. Tell him that for me? Please? Give her to Jimmy for me. Jimmy will take care of her, Jimmy loves her. Hold on to her for me. Read to her. Take her to the zoo. Be her friend.

KATE: But...

CARI LEE: Be Jimmy's friend.

KATE: Cari Lee...

CARI LEE: I know you think I'm trash and you got no reason to do anything for me ever, but if there's anything I can do for you in the future. Anything at all. It doesn't matter what. If I can help you out in any way at all, I will. Swear to god I will. Just do this one small thing for me and give Jimmy his girl.

(KATE *accepts the child)*

KATE: What's her name?

CARI LEE: Dale.

(CARI LEE *exits.* RICHARD *pulls another pocket watch out of his pocket, dangles it by its chain.)*

HELEN: Whose mortal clock is that?

(RICHARD *lifts his shirt revealing gauze and a clean bandage over his chest)*

HELEN: Oh no. No, no, no. Richard, no. You didn't.

RICHARD: Because I'll tell you, Helen...

HELEN: Have you looked at your mortal clock???

RICHARD: No. But I'll tell you, as soon as I realized you were almost gone from me, I knew—Helen, please look at me. Helen? If you're to die, please know that I do love you and I'm sorry I haven't let you know that you're a greater force than the universe and I am a stupid stupid man who can't change time but maybe I can change this. Helen, don't kill yourself, please. These stupid clocks are meaningless.

HELEN: If they were meaningless, you wouldn't be so terrified to look at your own.

RICHARD: What if...what if we could be tethered. What if I could give you my time?

(RICHARD *hands* HELEN *his pocket watch.*)

RICHARD: Please. Look. Tell me how much time I can give you. I'll figure it out. I'll make this work. I'll make it so we can be tethered. I will.

HELEN: You would give me your time?

RICHARD: I would give you every second.

(HELEN *looks at* RICHARD's *pocket watch. She looks at her pocket watch. She looks at them side by side. Dread...she closes the pocket watches.*)

HELEN: Oh my god.

RICHARD: What...?

HELEN: I'm so sorry, Richard.

(RICHARD *coughs, gasps.* HELEN *lifts his shirt to look at his bandaged chest.*)

RICHARD: When I pulled my mortal clock from my chest...the chain...caught. It wouldn't let go of my heart. And there was a terrible rip, and my heart...my heart...

HELEN: You shouldn't have done this.

RICHARD: But I had to! I had to try! I can't live without you, Helen.

HELEN: And I can't live without you.

RICHARD: So. We are tethered.

(Outside, JIMMY enters)

KATE: Cari Lee wanted me to give you your daughter. And. She wanted me to tell you that she says goodbye.

JIMMY: Goodbye? Where did she go?

KATE: I don't know. She didn't say.

JIMMY: When will she be back?

KATE: Jimmy, I don't think she's coming back.

JIMMY: What? She said that, that she's not coming back?

KATE: I'm sorry, Jimmy.

(KATE hands the baby to JIMMY)

JIMMY: What's the matter with her! How can she do this to me? I can't do this by myself! I don't know what I'm doing!

(Pause)

KATE: There's…books you can read?

JIMMY: Those books about babies are really intimidating. There's so much that can go wrong and there's all these rules. Babies are more complicated than a game of Dungeons and Dragons.

KATE: I'll teach you how to play D & D. It's not that hard.

JIMMY: *You* play Dungeons & Dragons?

KATE: I'm Rosalind the Dwarf.

JIMMY: You're a dwarf?

KATE: Dwarfs are fighters.

JIMMY: Sure.

KATE: No, really, they're fighters. They're good at fighting. They're just, y'know, they're small but they're strong. Do you want to play sometime?

JIMMY: Can I be dwarf?

KATE: Sure, but. But you strike me as more of the wizard-giant type.

JIMMY: I do? Is that good?

KATE: Yeah, that's good. Um. I babysit. If you're in a bind, and if I'm free. Or. If you just want somebody to go with you to the park. Or read to her. I can do that too.

JIMMY: You'll be going off to Harvard soon.

KATE: Well. What about you?

JIMMY: What about me?

KATE: What are you going to do now?

JIMMY: *(Looking at the baby)* I don't know what I'm doing.

KATE: That's okay.

JIMMY: Easy for you to say. You always know what you're doing. You're smart and you have a plan and you do it. I need to change her diaper.

KATE: See, you got a plan.

JIMMY: Got the next thirty minutes covered.

KATE: It takes thirty minutes to change a diaper?

JIMMY: I'm not very good at it.

KATE: Is it all right if I sit here for a little?

JIMMY: Sure. Why?

KATE: It's nice. Isn't it nice?

(HELEN *checks her pocket watch one last time. She stands and* RICHARD *reaches out for her, but he's too weak to stop her,)*

RICHARD: Please…Helen.

HELEN: I love you, Richard.

(HELEN *takes the shoebox and exits upstairs and* RICHARD *can only watch her go.)*

JIMMY: *(After a thought)* Yeah. It's nice.

(KATE *remains outside.* JIMMY *enters the shop.)*

JIMMY: Dad?

RICHARD: Jimmy. Tethered mortal clocks… *(Pained)*

JIMMY: Tethered mortal clocks? Dad, what's going on? Where's Mom?

RICHARD: Here. *(He puts a hand over his bandaged chest)* She is my heart.

(With his remaining strength, RICHARD *gets up. He checks the time on his pocket watch and then covers* JIMMY*'s ears with his hands. From upstairs in the apartment, the <u>sound</u> of a gunshot.* RICHARD *clutches his chest and blood pours from the bandage as his own chain-snagged heart tears apart. He crumples to the floor, dead.)*

(KATE looks through the shop window, alarmed at the gunshot. She sees…)

(JIMMY standing over the body of his dead father. He holds his daughter tightly.)

END OF ACT TWO

ACT THREE

Scene 1
The Past & Pending

(Early morning. KATE *is in the shop alone. She is studying* HELEN'*s book of mortal clockery.* KATE *is wearing glasses and using a magnifying glass.)*

(She feels a nosebleed coming on. She gets a Kleenex and jams in up her nostril. She looks out the shop window and sees...)

*(*KATE THE YOUNGER *wearing her cheerleading uniform, glasses. She also has a piece of Kleenex waded and shoved up her nostril, and in her hand, an acceptance letter from Harvard.)*

(They look at each other through the window, like a reflection.)

*(*KATE THE ELDER *exits the shop to stand/sit with* KATE THE YOUNGER *outside. They take the Kleenex out of their noses.)*

KATE THE ELDER: Harvard, huh? Off the waitlist, officially accepted. Congratulations.

KATE THE YOUNGER: Thanks. I guess.

KATE THE ELDER: You won't go to Harvard.

KATE THE YOUNGER: I won't?

KATE THE ELDER: You'll go to Northwestern. You'll
get a B A in Anthropology and Women's Studies, and
when you realize that is not practical, you will cripple
yourself with a Masters in English Literature. You
won't leave because what you thought was pity is
actually love, though it's easy to confuse the two. As
a side note, you will have one pre-marital, ohh, let's
call it a fling, tequila induced, with a math department
grad student named Steve, and you'll regret it—
mostly. Then, one morning, you'll wake up married,
and Jimmy will be sleeping there, next to you, snoring,
that gurgly-snoring that makes you think he's in
danger of drowning in spit, and you'll love him while
simultaneously wanting to elbow him in the head,
gently, because it's Saturday morning and you want to
sleep in too, and, no matter how many times you tell
Dale to put her dirty dishes directly in the dishwasher
because, guess what, it washes dishes, you'll hear her
cereal bowl and spoon clatter in the kitchen sink, and
those will be familiar morning sounds that, if you were
to have any life other than your own, you know you
would miss. You will get pregnant, ending in a late
miscarriage, leaving you sad with a vague sense that
you were supposed to meet somebody and missed a
long-standing appointment. And, all the wonderful
things you do have, you'll take for granted until the
day you're sitting here, wondering how it went so fast,
and how so easily it could all disappear.

(Pause)

KATE THE YOUNGER: Who's that Steve guy? Is he hot?

KATE THE ELDER: Steve is not your type.

KATE THE YOUNGER: Who's my type?

KATE THE ELDER: Jimmy. Or James Joyce.

KATE THE YOUNGER: James Joyce? Why? Do I get hit on
the head with a big rock between now and you?

KATE THE ELDER: Wait for it.

KATES: *(Together)* Now what?

Maybe we should—

You go first.

No, you go.

Stop it.

What color are you thinking of?

Indigo.

Burnt Sienna.

Purple Mountain's Majesty.

(CARI LEE enters from the shop carrying baby Dale—a Cliffs Notes repeat of the moment when KATE THE YOUNGER last saw CARI LEE. CARI LEE does not acknowledge KATE THE ELDER.)

CARI LEE: Hold on to her for me. Read to her. Take her to the zoo. Be her friend. If there's anything I can do for you in the future. If I can help you out in any way at all, I will. Just do this one small thing for me and give Jimmy his girl.

KATE THE YOUNGER: What's her name?

CARI LEE: Dale.

(KATE THE YOUNGER accepts the child. CARI LEE exits. Both KATES look at the baby.)

KATE THE ELDER: And that was that.

KATE THE YOUNGER: Jimmy said we should never talk about mortal clocks ever again.

KATE THE ELDER: I know.

KATE THE YOUNGER: Poor Mr and Mrs Wicker.

KATE THE YOUNGER: Good luck now that Cari Lee is back. Jimmy's still, like, totally in love with her.

KATE THE ELDER: No he's not.

KATE THE YOUNGER: I guess I never stop lying to myself, do I?

(KATE THE YOUNGER *exits with baby Dale, leaving just* KATE.)

(JIMMY *enters from upstairs. He sees the book open, looks at* KATE *outside. He closes the book.*)

JIMMY: How early did you get up?

KATE: Little bit after you came to bed. How did things go with Cari Lee's mortal clock?

JIMMY: Got the bleeding stopped.

KATE: Good. She was down here a long time.

RICHARD: We were talking.

(KATE *gives him a look*)

RICHARD: Are you seriously giving me "the look" about that?

KATE: What look?

JIMMY: "What look"? Come on, Kate.

KATE: You were down here together for a long time, that's all I meant. You haven't seen her in 18 years, I'm sure you were catching up. It's all right if she kissed you. Does Cari Lee still taste the same as you remember?

JIMMY: You don't know that she kissed me.

KATE: Did you kiss her back?

JIMMY: That's not fair. I never asked you if Steve Koviak kissed you back. (*Beat*) Oh that's right, you didn't know I knew about you and Math Department Steve.

KATE: I don't know what you're talking about.

(JIMMY *gives* KATE *"the look".*)

KATE: How long have you known about Steve?

JIMMY: Five years.

KATE: Wow. Okay. So awhile.

JIMMY: Yep.

KATE: May I explain?

JIMMY: Sure.

KATE: It was during those months before we were married, when we agreed it would be a good idea to "find ourselves".

JIMMY: That's what Steve said.

KATE: Steve told you.

JIMMY: He was going through a twelve step program. Oddly, his relationship with you was not his step nine confession. His confession was that he was the one who knocked the side-mirror off our car in the teachers' parking lot.

KATE: But I already knew about that.

JIMMY: He felt really bad about that side mirror. And we started talking. About you. And he said I was a lucky, lucky man to have you. And I said yes, I was a lucky man. And it just sorta came up. What happened, happened. It doesn't matter.

KATE: All right.

JIMMY: And, yes. Cari Lee kissed me last night.

KATE: I know.

JIMMY: You know.

KATE: I could smell her on you.

JIMMY: Is that like your super power?

KATE: Yes.

JIMMY: It didn't mean anything, Kate.

KATE: You don't have to pretend it didn't mean something. Of course it meant something.

(JIMMY looks at DALE's height markings on the wall.)

JIMMY: I knew Dale had a mortal clock in her head and I didn't want to see it. How could it happen to her, you know? She was the best thing to happen to me and how could anything bad possibly happen to her? Everything's fine. Everything's okay. And it's not. It never was. *(Takes DALE's mortal clock out of his pocket)* Dale's mortal clock.

KATE: Did you open it and look?

JIMMY: No. Should we look at it?

KATE: I don't know. Should we?

JIMMY: I don't know.

KATE: Yeah I don't know.

JIMMY: We probably should.

KATE: Maybe.

JIMMY: I mean, right?

KATE: Do we want to?

JIMMY: Do we?

(Pause. They do not open DALE's mortal clock.)

JIMMY: We should have a plan in case we don't like what we see. *(He gets the book. Drops it with a thud)*

KATE: Is that as far as your plan goes?

JIMMY: Yep.

KATE: Did something happen to Dale's mortal clock?

JIMMY: Time was stolen from it. But I don't know anything about tethered mortal clocks. My mom didn't leave anything in her book about how to fix tethered mortal clocks.

KATE: Tethered mortal clocks? Okay. *(She opens the book, searching)* You have a habit of skimming.

JIMMY: What are you talking about?

KATE: Books, newspapers, the *T V Guide.*

JIMMY: I do not skim, especially not the *T V Guide.*

(ROWAN enters the shop.)

KATE: This is why you're a wizard giant and I'm a dwarf. Where Wizard giants get scorched by dragons, dwarves don't give up. Even if they don't know what they're looking for. *(She gets the book of mortal clockery.)*

JIMMY: Don't you have to get ready for work?

KATE: Sick day. The substitute can show them Olivier's *Hamlet* or something I don't care. Hello, Rowan, how are you?

ROWAN: Great.

KATE: Great! *(She exits upstairs with the book.)*

ROWAN: I'm sorry I made a mess of Cari Lee's mortal clock.

JIMMY: Don't worry about it.

ROWAN: It's an amazing thing, though, a mortal clock, isn't it? The guts packed in there with the gears and springs and movements.

JIMMY: We don't talk about mortal clocks outside this shop. It's best if people don't know.

ROWAN: I think people would want to know.

JIMMY: They would, yes. But we all live with certain assumptions and one of those assumptions is that we will still be here tomorrow. Nobody expects to live forever, but nobody expects to die in the next ten minutes. This business with mortal clocks. It stays here.

ROWAN: All right.

JIMMY: Are you okay with this?

ROWAN: Yes, Mr Wicker. *(Pause)* I wanted to take your daughter out tonight. For coffee. Or for dinner, like. If it's all right with you.

JIMMY: Yeah sure fine.

ROWAN: Oh. Great. Thank you.

(ROWAN goes back to work. JIMMY lifts his head from his work)

JIMMY: I'm sorry, what?

ROWAN: What?

JIMMY: What did you say?

ROWAN: Oh. I. I asked if it's all right if I take your daughter out. Earlier in the week, I asked Dale if she would like to go out tonight.

JIMMY: "Go out"?

ROWAN: For coffee. Or dinner. Or such.

JIMMY: You want to take my daughter on a date?

ROWAN: We're not calling it that, but—

JIMMY: What are you calling it?

ROWAN: A coat rack. It would just be coffee or a dinner, like.

JIMMY: Don't take this the wrong way, Rowan. You're a nice guy. But under no circumstances do I want you dating my daughter. Is that clear?

ROWAN: Very clear, Mr Wicker. …May I ask why not?

JIMMY: I don't know how they do things in Ireland, but twenty-two year olds—

ROWAN: Twenty-one.

JIMMY: —don't generally—twenty-one year olds—don't go on dates with seventeen year olds.

ROWAN: She's eighteen.

JIMMY: She's too young for you.

(CARI LEE *enters from upstairs.*)

CARI LEE: Jimmybear, when are we gonna *do it,* when are we gonna make a baby?

JIMMY: Can I talk to you outside?

CARI LEE: I don't wanna go outside Rowan can go outside.

JIMMY: Rowan can stay in. *You* can come outside.

CARI LEE: I *can.* But I'm not gonna.

JIMMY: (*Giving money to* ROWAN) Rowan, would you do me a favor—

ROWAN: Grande skim no whip toffee nut mocha.

JIMMY: Get something for yourself.

CARI LEE: And I'll have coffee thanks. You rock. Like Bono.

(ROWAN *exits.* CARI LEE *jumps on* JIMMY)

JIMMY: Cari Lee, stop.

CARI LEE: You started my mortal clock and now I'm *dying.* Have we learned nothing from the movie *Beaches*?

(DALE *enters from upstairs with her backpack.*)

CARI LEE: Dale, tell your dad to have sex with me.

JIMMY: She's kidding.

CARI LEE: I'm not kidding.

JIMMY: Wait—hold up—we need to talk. Rowan mentioned something about tonight, about going out tonight. It's fine if you're friends with him, but I don't like the idea of you going on a date.

DALE: It's not a date. It's a coat rack.

JIMMY: I don't understand what that means. And I don't like it. You're not going out with him.

DALE: You can't do that.

JIMMY: Welllll I can and I just did.

(KATE *will enter from upstairs with the book and observe.*)

DALE: I'm going out tonight.

JIMMY: No you're not.

DALE: Here's an idea, Dad: how about you seal me in an airtight shatter proof glass box so nothing happens to me ever. I'll just stay in my little box and I'll use up my air until I suffocate and die.

JIMMY: You're not going out with Rowan.

CARI LEE: Oh, yeah, Lucky Charms? He's cute. Man, I remember my first real date with you Jimmybear, a date-date, not just, like, random play.

JIMMY: Uhh—I'd prefer if you didn't—

CARI LEE: Jimmybear took me *bowling* which was fine 'cept we couldn't keep our hands off each other even with three fingers in a ten pound ball. Then later we got hot in the back of his dad's car and I'm like "you wanna" and he's all "I dunno" and I'm all "c'mon man" and he's all "but I don't have protection" and I'm all "you can't get pregnant in a Buick." The moral of this story is don't do it in the back seat of a Buick as its contraceptive powers are totally overrated. (*To* JIMMY) I'll be upstairs if you need me. (*She exits.*)

DALE: I'm gonna walk to school. I don't need a ride. And just so you know, Rowan's really nice. And I like him. And he listens to me. And he's had a hard time too, with his mom, and...and when I'm around him I don't feel like I'm dying.

(DALE *exits the shop.* ROWAN *enters with coffee*)

ROWAN: Dale, hi. I talked to your dad…

DALE: I know.

ROWAN: Maybe some other time, right?

DALE: Right. …Soon, I hope.

ROWAN: Um, will you just wait here a moment. If you're not in a hurry. I'll be back out.

(DALE *waits outside the shop.* ROWAN *enters the shop with coffee.*)

ROWAN: They were out of the toffee nut flavor so it's just a regular mocha. And coffee for Cari Lee.

KATE: Rowan, wait.

(KATE *gestures for* JIMMY *to talk to* ROWAN.)

JIMMY: What?

(KATE *repeats the gesture.*)

JIMMY: What?

(KATE *repeats her gesture*)

KATE: You let him know he can take our daughter on a date.

JIMMY: No.

KATE: Why not?

JIMMY: Because he's a *guy*.

KATE: Yes.

JIMMY: I don't want her dating. Anybody. Ever.

KATE: Jimmy.

(KATE *nudges* JIMMY *to* ROWAN. *Pause*)

JIMMY: Rowan. About tonight… If you're. If you're looking for something to do tonight. There's a place in Highwood. Place called Pops For Champagne. They have jazz starting at eight. Dale loves jazz. They don't card at the door—just—don't buy alcohol. No alcohol.

KATE: Why don't you give him some money for the cover charge?

JIMMY: What?

KATE: Give him some money.

ROWAN: Oh, you don't have to.

KATE: We insist.

(JIMMY *gets his wallet, gives cash to* ROWAN.)

ROWAN: Thank you, Mr Wicker.

KATE: Why don't you take the rest of the day off, Rowan.

JIMMY: Oh fer—! go. Just go. Get outta here. Go.

ROWAN: Are you sure now?

JIMMY: Yes. Go away please.

ROWAN: I'll treat her well. She's a very nice girl.

JIMMY: All right.

(ROWAN *exits the shop and stands outside with* DALEe. *We can't hear them, but see them through the shop window. He tells her the good news and She looks into the shop with a wave of thanks to her parents. They remain outside, talking together, enjoying each other's company.*)

KATE: That was very nice of you, Jimmy.

JIMMY: Oh, it was my pleasure.

(KATE *opens the book.*)

KATE: Here: "Mother and child, tethered, bound by chain for time eternal."

JIMMY: Right.

KATE: I could give Dale some of my time.

JIMMY: What?

KATE: If a mother and child are tethered…is what I'm saying. I'm her mother.

JIMMY: Kate—okay, yes, mother and child are tethered, but only in the womb. And second, you're not... biologically, I mean, you haven't ever been connected that way. A tether is a physical connection.

KATE: I've rocked her to sleep, bandaged her scraped knees, tied her shoes. Hugged her when she was scared or sad, ran alongside her bicycle after we threw away the training wheels.

JIMMY: That's not the kind of physical connection that matters. Biology aside, time only transferred from Dale's mortal clock to Cari Lee's because Dale hadn't been born yet. There is no tether beyond a literal physical blood and body connection between mother and child.

KATE: You know that for sure?

JIMMY: It's what my mother told me.

KATE: Did your mother and father love each other?

JIMMY: No.

KATE: No?

JIMMY: They never seemed to like each other very much.

KATE: But after all those years and all the people your mother met through an extraordinary lifetime, all the people she could have ended with ... she ended with your father. They died together. What if your mother and father were tethered? What if? Jimmy, that's all we got. Those what if's, what could be's, if only's. Cari Lee dropped Dale into my arms, and I held her, and I knew I could love this sad little girl more than anything. Dale is my child. And she is my heart.

(CARI LEE *enters from upstairs, listens.*)

JIMMY: You do realize where your own mortal clock is, don't you? (*He places his hand over* KATE's *heart.*) Chain wrapped round and round that tricky little muscle. Come here, I want you to look at this. *(He flips to a different page in the book.)* See. To get your mortal clock, I'll have to drill through your ribcage. And then… extract the clock…and then cauterize it. It can be done, but. I don't know if I can do it.

CARI LEE: Are you out of your minds?

KATE: I want to give some of my time to Dale.

CARI LEE: You can't do that. Jimmy, she can't do that. I'm Dale's mom, only I can do that, if it can be done at all, which it probably can't. And what about me, man? Don't you wanna make a baby with me?

KATE: What now?

CARI LEE: *(To KATE)* Don't you want a baby?

JIMMY: Cari Lee—

CARI LEE: My stupid mortal clock is ticking and if we're going to do this, we have to do it very very soon or it won't happen at all. And this time in me isn't even mine, it belongs to Dale and I'm not gonna waste it and you shouldn't waste it either. Ten months.

KATE: Did you start her mortal clock?

JIMMY: Yes.

KATE: To make a baby?

JIMMY: No, Kate.

CARI LEE: You never said no.

JIMMY: I didn't say yes.

KATE: Why didn't you say no?

JIMMY: There was a lot going on last night!

CARI LEE: You never said no and that's like a yes.

JIMMY: It's a generous offer, and thank you. But no.

CARI LEE: I wanna help you replace Dale.

JIMMY: We can't replace Dale. She's not like a broken coffee mug we can replace.

CARI LEE: But I want to.

JIMMY: Cari Lee: no.

(Pause)

CARI LEE: So that's it? I'm offering the rest of my life to make you two happy and you don't give a crap about me. I got ten months. To do what? To do what? What am I supposed to do, Jimmy?

JIMMY: We're going to fix this.

CARI LEE: You can't fix this! You broke me, you broke Dale, and now you're gonna break Kate.

JIMMY: If I can figure the rate of transfer to be one equals one, I can transfer entire years in tact. Probably.

CARI LEE: *Probably?* Kate. Please don't do this. It's gonna end badly.

JIMMY: I need your help.

CARI LEE: No way, man. You are nuts. *(To* KATE*)* And you are nuts. Clearly you two are perfect for each other.

*(*JIMMY *gets* DALE's *mortal clock. Holds it out)*

CARI LEE: Is that Dale's mortal clock?

JIMMY: Yeah.

CARI LEE: Did you look?

*(*JIMMY *gives* CARI LEE *and* KATE *both a look of "Are you ready?" They are ready.)*

(He opens it and they look. Any hope they had drains away. DALE *will be dead in five days.)*

(Their responses to the bad news are individual and personal. Denial and grief and sadness and fear and resolve.)

(They will do anything to triumph over this terrible mortal clock.)

(Outside the shop, DALE *and* ROWAN *talk together. They enjoy each other's company on a nice spring day.)*

Scene 2
The Dwarf & The Giant

(Later that evening. JIMMY *and* CARI LEE *in the shop, He is mixing up some potion. Bottles and liquids and powders. He consults the book of mortal clockery, preparing for the extraction.)*

JIMMY: Pass the Locksbreath.

CARI LEE: Which one is that?

JIMMY: Green bottle.

*(*CARI LEE *passes the bottle.* JIMMY *adds a pinch. Consults the book)*

JIMMY: Here, keep stirring this. *(He preps his tools: the drill, pliers, scary sharp hook.)*

CARI LEE: *(Stirring)* Smells like ass. Kate has to drink this?

JIMMY: Yeah.

CARI LEE: You remember that guy sophomore year who drank a pint of pickle juice, cayenne pepper, and toothpaste, and then puked it down the main stairwell?

JIMMY: That was me.

CARI LEE: Oh, right, that was you.

JIMMY: Won twenty bucks. No regrets. After I add this, keep stirring, but slow it down. *(He adds a drop of something to the mixture.)* All right. *(Referring to the book)* Did that. Did that. Did that. Did that. Did that.

CARI LEE: What would you do if you only had ten months to live?

JIMMY: Um. I don't know. Maybe I'd... build a boat.

CARI LEE: "Build a boat." Wow.

JIMMY: Why did you ask if you were going to be critical?

CARI LEE: I didn't know you'd be so boring.

JIMMY: I'd build a boat, sail around the world.

CARI LEE: You can't build a boat and sail around the world in ten months.

JIMMY: You're just full of nay-saying, aren't you.

CARI LEE: I am not! Ten months. That's all I got. And here I am. Stirring ass-flavored kool ade, waiting for my daughter to die.

JIMMY: This is going to work.

CARI LEE: What if you yank Kate's mortal clock out of her chest and you look at it and she has, like, three years? Or two years? Or one year? Or seven months? Or seven seconds? She might not have time to give to Dale. She might not have anything but a hole in her chest and then what?

JIMMY: You gotta cool it on the negativity if we're going to get through this.

CARI LEE: Jimmy, you are confusing negativity with practicality! *(She gasps, covers her own mouth, repulsed by the adult wisdom that just came out of her mouth.)*

JIMMY: Wow.

CARI LEE: What's happening to me?

JIMMY: You're getting older.

(KATE enters like a boxing champ. She wears a robe and clothes that could handle a blood stain or two)

KATE: Let's do this! I'm ready! Let's go!

JIMMY: Almost ready.

CARI LEE: Smell this.

(KATE *smells the liquid mixture, gags*)

KATE: What is that?

JIMMY: You're going to have to drink that.

KATE: Oh yay.

JIMMY: It's a mixture of a few different things. This stuff *(Picks up a bottle)* will loosen the chain around your heart—the last thing I want is to have the chain snag your heart when I pull it out. And this stuff… *(Adds a liquid)* …will dull the pain of the drill. This stuff will prep the chest cavity for penetration and intrusion. But there's nothing I can give to take away the pain of time. It might hurt. It might be horrible. Are you sure you want to do this?

KATE: I'll make it through. I'll be all right.

JIMMY: Well I'm glad you think it'll be all right, because I'm scared as hell.

KATE: I want to do this, Jimmy.

(JIMMY *holds out the mug*)

JIMMY: Drink this and there's no turning back. Once the chain is loose, it has to come out.

CARI LEE: Chug, chug, chug, chug, chug.

(KATE *drinks, keeps it down.*)

JIMMY: Gotta wait a little, let it soak through. You're going to start feeling…

KATE: What?

JIMMY: You'll just have to let me know how it feels when you start feeling it. *(He checks his watch, glances*

out the window) Dale and Rowan should be back by
now.

KATE: It's not that late.

JIMMY: They should be home soon. It's getting late.

KATE: I don't think we have to worry about Dale and
Rowan. They're out having a great time, and she *finally*
wore that dress I got her for Christmas. Didn't she look
great?

JIMMY: She looked nice. She looked happy.

CARI LEE: I bet they're gonna do it.

(JIMMY and KATE look at CARI LEE.)

CARI LEE: If I only had five days to live, I would do it.
Especially if I hadn't done it before. And his accent is
hot.

KATE: I know, right? What is it about Irish men? Like
if I met James Joyce, I'd go to town on him. *(As if this is
the sexiest thing in the world:)* He wore an eye patch.

*(JIMMY looks at KATE. She is clearly succumbing to the
potion—but still. CARI LEE is amused.)*

JIMMY: Ohhh kay.

KATE: Baby, don't be jealous, James Joyce lives all the
way over in Paris. And he's dead. I wanna kiss your
face so hard your shoes fall off.

(KATE kisses JIMMY)

JIMMY: How ya feeling?

KATE: I don't feel anything yet I really don't think its
working is it working I think I need more.

JIMMY: You don't need any more.

KATE: Feel my heart. My little dwarf heart is pounding
like mad.

JIMMY: Your little dwarf heart. *(He kisses KATE)*

CARI LEE: Get a room.

(KATE *embraces* CARI LEE.)

KATE: I love you so much.

CARI LEE: Yeah?

KATE: My love for you is like a box of sixty-four crayons with the little crayon sharpener in the side. *(She breathes deeply, a sense of euphoria.)* Ohhhhhh god.

JIMMY: That's the chain loosening around her heart.

KATE: Holy moly, you gotta drink some of that stuff, it's like totally unreal. It's like... *(Total euphoria)* ... ohhhhh.... oh yeah.

CARI LEE: That ass Kool Ade is awesome.

JIMMY: All right, how about you lie down now.

KATE: You, sir, are very attractive.

JIMMY: Thank you.

KATE: You're welcome. *(Regarding the coat rack)* Has this always been here?

JIMMY: Pretty much always.

KATE: It's really neat, I really like it. You wanna do something, Jimmy, like anything, like we could play D & D and then you can ravish me.

JIMMY: That sounds fun but we have to take care of your mortal clock first.

KATE: Oh right that right that yeah.

JIMMY: Lie down. Breathe slowly, slowly.

KATE: I love you, Jimmy.

JIMMY: I love you, Kate.

KATE: Ohhhh I'm sorry. I'm getting sleepy.

JIMMY: Stay awake, okay? You can't go to sleep yet. Kate? Keep her awake, I gotta get the drill ready.

CARI LEE: Kate? KATE!

KATE: WHAT!

CARI LEE: You gotta stay awake. Let's sing a song to stay awake.

(CARI LEE starts singing a TvV theme song at KATE— maybe the theme from "Cheers" or "Growing Pains"— trying to get her to join in and stay awake.)

JIMMY: Here, take these towels. Put these on. *(He gives CARI LEE a pair of latex gloves.)* Kate, you still awake?

(KATE gives a thumb up.)

JIMMY: What I need you to do is after I pull out the mortal clock, you need to hold these towels over the hole in her chest until I can pour the sealant and cauterizer. Press down hard. Hard. Got it?

CARI LEE: Got it.

JIMMY: And you may have to press a finger down on—

CARI LEE: Let me know when we get there.

JIMMY: You gotta be at the ready when it comes out, she can't lose too much blood. Stand right over here, okay.

(JIMMY climbs on top and straddles KATE.)

KATE: Hey baby.

JIMMY: Hey sweetheart. You ready to do this?

KATE: Do it.

JIMMY: Okay. Here goes. Ready. The drill's not supposed to hurt.

(JIMMY positions the drill on KATE's chest. He cranks a couple quick cranks. It may very well be messy.)

KATE: Gaaahaha!

JIMMY: Oh god—does it hurt?!

KATE: *(Laughing now)* Tickles.

(And JIMMY'*s through. He removes the drill.)*

JIMMY: Cover that, cover that.

CARI LEE: Cover it now?

JIMMY: Yeah!

CARI LEE: You said not until after you pull the mortal clock—

JIMMY: Cover it! Forget what I said, cover it!

*(*CARI LEE *covers* KATE'*s chest.)*

CARI LEE: What's wrong?

JIMMY: The hole's not big enough. Oh… Okay. Kate?

KATE: Yeah.

JIMMY: Hold on a minute. *(He goes to his tools.)*

KATE: Where'm I gonna go, ha ha.

CARI LEE: Uh, Jimmy. This is starting to bleed a little.

JIMMY: A little *a lot* or a little a little?

CARI LEE: It's not a lot, but it's seeping a little.

*(*JIMMY *grabs an auger to widen the hole.)*

CARI LEE: I'm getting a little light headed.

JIMMY: What?

CARI LEE: Think I'm gonna faint.

JIMMY: Don't faint.

CARI LEE: Yep I'm gonna faint.

JIMMY: No, Cari Lee, don't!

*(*CARI LEE *faints on top of* KATE'*s mid-section…)*

KATE: Oooof!

(Leaving KATE'*s chest hole unattended and spurting)*

JIMMY: Cari Lee!

CARI LEE: Whauh?

JIMMY: Get off!

CARI LEE: I'm okay.

KATE: I can't…I can't breathe well. Can't…really breathe.

JIMMY: *(Giving* KATE *a towel)* Kate, can you hold this on your chest?

KATE: Yeah I'll just do everything myself.

JIMMY: Press down. Hold it.

(JIMMY *pulls* CARI LEE *off* KATE. *He'll put her on the floor.)*

JIMMY: You okay?

CARI LEE: I'm sorry.

JIMMY: Don't be sorry.

CARI LEE: The blood, man.

(JIMMY *returns to* KATE. *He pours some liquid from a bottle onto her chest, and then cranks the auger in the hole. She winces.)*

JIMMY: You might feel this.

KATE: Pressure in my chest.

JIMMY: That'll pass. You're doing good. You're doing really good. …That's gonna have to be big enough. Cari Lee!

CARI LEE: What?

JIMMY: I need you. I need your help. You okay?

CARI LEE: I'm just like totally great all the time.

JIMMY: Can you get up? Get up.

(JIMMY *grabs his tools and works quickly but carefully to pull the chain and pocket watch from* KATE's *chest,* CARI LEE *gets off the floor, woozy still.)*

JIMMY: The chain is really loose.

KATE: Aaaahhhh....

JIMMY: Kate, we're almost there. Almost there. Cari Lee: get the towels and get ready. Ready?

CARI LEE: Ready.

JIMMY: Okay. Free and clear. Towels! Towels!

(CARI LEE *presses the towels over* KATE's *chest.* JIMMY *sets the pocket watch aside and gets some bottles.*)

JIMMY: Lift.

(CARI LEE *lifts the towels and he pours a couple different liquids to fill the hole in her chest.*)

JIMMY: Press down and hold it there.

CARI LEE: This good?

JIMMY: Yeah, just hold it. Easy as pie.

CARI LEE: Crazy-ass pie.

JIMMY: Kate? ...KATE!

KATE: Ohhhh I never wanna do that again.

JIMMY: Here, let me take over towel duty so I can check it.

CARI LEE: How's it look.

JIMMY: Looks good. Looks great. This won't even need a bandage. Here, take over, wipe that off.

(CARI LEE *holds the towels and* JIMMY *gets* KATE's *pocket watch.*)

JIMMY: Look what I got.

(JIMMY *shows* KATE *the pocket watch.*)

KATE: It's beautiful.

JIMMY: It is. (*He opens* KATE's *pocket watch to look.*)

CARI LEE: Kate has time to spare?

JIMMY: Yeah. Here will you hand me Dale's mortal clock? *(He puts the pocket watches next to each other on the table. He crosses the watch chains to the other watch.)*

CARI LEE: Do you have any idea what you're doing?

JIMMY: I can do this.

(JIMMY begins carefully fiddling with the watches. Outside the shop, DALE and ROWAN enter.)

ROWAN: I should've brought you back sooner.

DALE: *(Finishing her yawn)* No, I'm sorry. I'm not tired.

ROWAN: I have a confession to make.

DALE: What?

ROWAN: Tonight was my first jazz quartet.

DALE: Did you like it? Did you like the band?

ROWAN: Very much.

DALE: They were really good. The band on the schedule for next Friday, now they're great. I don't have their C D but I heard them on W D C B and I called the D J and he told me who they were and then I meant to download their stuff but the computer froze, and then I went to see if the library had their C D but they didn't. So I went home. …And then my head fell off. …I'm sorry, that story was going nowhere, it needed an ending.

ROWAN: Then that *is* a good story if your head did fall off at the end!

DALE: I know, it was, like, crazy, I couldn't believe it.

ROWAN: I had a good time.

DALE: Me too. Yeah. I had a great time.

ROWAN: Me too.

DALE: Yeah. Yeah. Me too.

ROWAN: Yeah.

(Awkward)

DALE: Did you want to kiss me because you totally can if you want.

ROWAN: Your dad keeps a baseball bat in the shop, I worry he'd batter my skull for kissing his daughter.

DALE: I wouldn't let him do that.

(DALE and ROWAN are about to kiss.)

JIMMY: Okay. Now Dale's mortal clock...

(JIMMY fiddles with DALE's pocket watch. DALE pulls away from ROWAN.)

ROWAN: Something wrong?

DALE: I just got dizzy.

ROWAN: Are you all right?

JIMMY: Almost...

DALE: My head. Hurts.

ROWAN: You've gone a bit pale.

JIMMY: There!

(DALE cries, pained, collapses into ROWAN's arms)

ROWAN: Dale? Dale!

CARI LEE: *(Looking out the window)* Jimmy.

JIMMY: I'm busy!

CARI LEE: Dale's out there, something's wrong.

JIMMY: What—I can't stop here—go check on her.

(CARI LEE runs to the door.)

CARI LEE: What happened?

ROWAN: She said she was dizzy and her head hurt.

CARI LEE: *(Shouting to JIMMY through the open shop door)* She said she was dizzy and her head hurt!

JIMMY: Is she conscious?

CARI LEE: Is she conscious?

ROWAN: No.

CARI LEE: *(Shouting to* JIMMY*)* No!

JIMMY: Okay. Okay. Let me know if she wakes up! *(To himself)*...It's all right. It's all right. No problem.

ROWAN: What's happening?

CARI LEE: Kate is giving Dale more time.

JIMMY: Kate? KATE!

KATE: Huhn.

JIMMY: You okay? ...KATE!

KATE: Whah?

JIMMY: Do you feel anything yet?

KATE: No.

ROWAN: She's awake.

CARI LEE: *(Shouting to* JIMMY*)* She's awake!

JIMMY: This is gonna work. Here we go.

*(*JIMMY *cranks a pocket watch. A terrible ratcheting noise)*

*(*DALE *and* KATE *writhe, pained.* KATE *howls.)*

*(*CARI LEE *goes to* KATE *in the shop.)*

JIMMY: One year.

*(*JIMMY *cranks a pocket watch. A terrible ratcheting noise.)*

*(*DALE *and* KATE *writhe, pained.)*

JIMMY: Two years.

CARI LEE: *(To* KATE*)* You're doing great. Just hold on. Here, squeeze my hand.

*(*JIMMY *cranks a pocket watch. A terrible ratcheting noise.)*

*(*DALE *and* KATE *writhe, pained.)*

JIMMY: Three years.

ROWAN: WHAT'S GOING ON IN THERE?

(JIMMY *cranks a pocket watch. A terrible ratcheting noise.*)

(DALE *and* KATE *writhe, pained.*)

JIMMY: Four years. That's all. That's enough.

KATE: You haven't given her enough. Keep going.

(JIMMY cranks a pocket watch. A terrible ratcheting noise.

(DALE *and* KATE *writhe, pained.*)

JIMMY: Five years.

KATE: Keep going!

(JIMMY *cranks a pocket watch. A terrible ratcheting noise.*)

(DALE *and* KATE *writhe, pained.*)

JIMMY: Six years.

KATE: Keep going!

JIMMY: No.

KATE: Just a few more years.

CARI LEE: Kate, don't.

KATE: I want to.

(JIMMY *cranks a pocket watch. A terrible ratcheting noise.*)

(DALE *and* KATE *writhe, pained.*)

JIMMY: Seven years.

KATE: More.

JIMMY: No more!

KATE: You haven't given her enough!

JIMMY: The spring is way too tight, I can't!

CARI LEE: Kate: you've given enough.

KATE: GIVE HER MORE TIME! I know you can do it.

(JIMMY *cranks a pocket watch. A terrible ratcheting noise.*)

(DALE *and* KATE *writhe, pained.*)

(*And then a different noise—something ominous*)

JIMMY: No!!!! No!!! STOP!

(KATE *shakes and screams in pain.* CARI LEE *tries to hold her down. Outside,* DALE *writhes and howls.* JIMMY *removes his shaking hands from the pocket watches.* KATE *and* DALE *stop moving. Silence. Then* DALE *wakes.*)

DALE: I'm living. I have time!

(DALE *runs into the shop, but halts when she sees the aftermath.* ROWAN *looks in through the shop window.* CARI LEE *looks at* DALE. JIMMY *is devastated.* KATE *is dead*)

Scene 3
Yesterday, Today, & Tomorrow

(JIMMY *alone in the shop. He holds* KATE's *mortal clock.* CARI LEE *enters with her mortal clock.*)

CARI LEE: You know how I said I wanted to go skydiving before I died? I never went skydiving. I never rode a horse on a beach at dawn. And I never became an urban graffiti artist like Banksy. All these things I wanted to do before I died and I didn't do *any of them* and I'm running out of time.

JIMMY: You knew exactly how much time you have left.

CARI LEE: I know! But, like, there was a lot of good stuff on T V.

(*Pause*)

I made a mistake, Jimmy. You gotta stop this thing. I don't want to die.

JIMMY: I can't.

CARI LEE: You gotta stop it, man. You did it once.

JIMMY: I can't, Cari Lee.

CARI LEE: Come on, man.

JIMMY: I'm sorry. My hands don't work on mortal clocks. I'm sorry.

(CARI LEE *opens her mortal clock and looks at it. She leaves the open mortal clock in front of* JIMMY. *She exits outside the shop to the bench. He closes her mortal clock, unable to look at it.* DALE *enters from outside with a small airmail package. She approaches* CARI LEE *on the bench.*)

DALE: Rowan and I are going to see a movie tonight. You wanna come?

CARI LEE: Am I gonna have to sit next to you and Kissyface McGuillitcutty slobbering all over each other?

DALE: It's not really a make-out movie.

CARI LEE: What movie?

DALE: On The Waterfront. There's a Marlon Brando festival at the Wilmette Theatre. I don't know, it's supposed to be a good movie. Have you seen it?

CARI LEE: Yeah.

DALE: We could see something else if you've already seen it.

CARI LEE: It's worth seeing again.

DALE: So you wanna?

CARI LEE: Yeah. That would be really nice.

(CARI LEE *looks closely at* DALE.)

DALE: Why are you looking at me like that?

CARI LEE: I like your face.

(*The phone rings inside the shop.* JIMMY *does not move to answer it.* DALE *enters the shop and answers the phone.*)

DALE: Wicker's Watch & Clock Repair.

*

Hi, Mrs Herman. *(Covers phone)* Dad? *(No response)*
*
Dad can't come to the phone right now, but I can take a
message.
*
I'll ask him, but I know for sure he likes your apple
strudel.
*
We're doing okay. Thanks.
*
Okay, bye. *(Hangs up. Off* JIMMY's *look)* She thought
I was grandma when I answered the phone. Here, I
stopped by the post office on the way back from the
library.

*(*DALE *hands* JIMMY *the airmail package.)*

JIMMY: Germany...

DALE: Rowan said he'd be here in a half hour. He went
to pick up the two mantle clocks from Mrs Boyle.

JIMMY: All right.

DALE: You should come out with me and Rowan and
Cari Lee tonight. We're going to see a movie, maybe
get some ice cream after.

JIMMY: Oh. You all have fun.

DALE: I want you to come with us.

JIMMY: Not tonight.

DALE: Dad. Please.

JIMMY: Let me think about it.

*(*JIMMY *exits upstairs with* KATE's *mortal clock.* DALE *opens*
HELEN's *book of mortal clockery. Outside the shop,* HELEN
enters and peers through the window. She enters the shop.
DALE *and* HELEN *look at each other a moment.)*

HELEN: Let me see your hands. *(She approaches* DALE.*)*
Let me see your hands.

(DALE *holds out her hands.* HELEN *examines them with clinical precision*)

HELEN: It would behoove you to abstain from snacking on your fingernails. Your hands are very special, Dale. Do you know why they're so special?

DALE: Why?

HELEN: Because you have hands for more advanced work. (*Reading from her book:*) "Bone and blood and heart and vein. This, the contents of a mortal clock, the intricacy wherefore dictated by the induvidual."

DALE: You—nevermind.

HELEN: What?

DALE: You spelled individual wrong.

HELEN: Nobody's perfect. (*Hands* DALE *a pen*) Fix it.

(DALE *fixes the spelling error*)

DALE: I-N-D-*I*-V-I...

HELEN: D-U-A-L. Ah ha. Continue reading here...

DALE: "For every body is one mortal clock. For every stick of bone and cup of blood, Rope of artery, band of sinew and gr...?"

HELEN: Grizzle. (*Reading:*) "Such mortal fodder corresponds to the inlaid mortal components. Components must be compacted exactly as shown, for proper function and display." Someone must have loved you very much to have given you so much time.

DALE: I'm a thief. I stole every second she had.

HELEN: You didn't steal anything, Dale. She gave you life. She wouldn't have it any other way. Mothers are odd creatures. (*Approaching the window, looks at* CARI LEE *outside*) Especially that one.

DALE: I don't want her to die. (*She picks up* CARI LEE's *mortal clock. Looking at the engraving*) Cari Lee. (*A moment)* My hands can stop her mortal clock. *(Then, realizing)* My hands can stop my mortal clock.

HELEN: Yes.

(DALE looks at her hands, realizing the wonderful/dreadful power she has.)

HELEN: But, as you know, there are consequences.

(JIMMY enters from upstairs. He does not see HELEN. He walks right by her.)

HELEN: You need to encourage him to keep living. Will you do that for your father?

DALE: Yes.

(JIMMY looks through the window at CARI LEE outside on the bench, triggering a memory.)

YOUNG JIMMY: *(Offstage)* Cari Lee!

CARI LEE: Jimmybear!

(Outside, YOUNG JIMMY enters. JIMMY will exit the shop to watch.)

YOUNG JIMMY: Where have you been, Cari Lee?! You said you'd meet me at the bike racks. We have an appointment, I don't want to be late. Don't you want to know if it's a boy or a girl?

CARI LEE: It's a girl.

YOUNG JIMMY: How do you know?

CARI LEE: I just know, man. It's just something I have a sense about.

YOUNG JIMMY: Are you sure it's a girl?

CARI LEE: Yeah.

YOUNG JIMMY: Oh.

CARI LEE: What?

YOUNG JIMMY: I don't know anything about girls.

CARI LEE: Yeah, no kidding.

YOUNG JIMMY: You think she'll like baseball? Can I force a girl to like baseball or is that bad parenting? Can I ask you a serious question?

CARI LEE: Okay.

YOUNG JIMMY: When are you gonna get fat?

CARI LEE: Are you still gonna love me when I'm five hundred pounds.

YOUNG JIMMY: Yeah. Jeez. You're going to be somebody's mom.

CARI LEE: What's so funny? I'll be a good mom. *(Pause)* Why are you looking at me like that.

YOUNG JIMMY: If I stop looking, I'm afraid I'll forget what you look like.

CARI LEE: You can't forget me, man. I'm stuck to you like glue, forever and ever.

HELEN: *(Referring to her book of mortal clockery)* This is yours now. Please do some rewriting. I'm ashamed of how wrong I was. We're not tethered by flesh or bone or chain. It's love. Love gives time. *(She opens the shop door.)* Don't you two have a doctors appointment?

YOUNG JIMMY: We're going. We won't be late.

HELEN: And after your appointment? What are your intentions for this evening, Jimmy.

YOUNG JIMMY: We're going to study.

HELEN: If you two insist on studying, I won't stop you. But there is a full moon tonight. Your father and I used to sit on that crumbling concrete pier at Elder Street Beach when there was a full moon, and all the stars over the water. I would recommend the lake tonight. You can study tomorrow.

(YOUNG JIMMY *holds out his hand to* CARI LEE. *She takes it and they exit.* HELEN *approaches* JIMMY *sitting with* KATE's *pocket watch.* JIMMY *doesn't see* HELEN.)

HELEN: You don't see those stars anymore, blanked out by the harsh sun and sleepless city lights. Do you remember when you could see them? Even if you can't see them now, you know in your heart they're still there, where they've always been. Where they always will be. Look up, Jimmy. Do you see? All those stars in all those galaxies, stretching into infinite time, tangled and tethered together, always together.

(JIMMY *looks up to the sky, eyes searching, as if he somehow heard her.* HELEN *exits.* JIMMY *holds* KATE's *pocket watch to his chest. The lights fade, the clocks tick tock, and the WATCH & CLOCK REPAIR sign glows until, at last, it winks out.*)

END OF PLAY